Praise for the Liptons' *Walking Easy* series

"Very thorough, organized and concise. A buy, by all means."**—Barbara Sylvia, *Senior Scene***

"Your book helped us with all the things it seemed we had to learn in a foreign country . . . I can't tell you how valuable it proved to be."**—B.D., Albuquerque, New Mexico**

"We have taken our groups on many of the walks the Liptons describe, so we fully appreciate the accuracy and care they have given to their writing."**—Richard Newman, Study Tours Abroad**

"It's very easy to read and very informative . . . I recommend the Liptons' book."**—Rex Burnett, *SwissTrek***

"The directions are excellent. This was our first [alpine] walking attempt, and I was very reassured to know we were on the right track."**—J.F., Sunrise, Florida**

walking easy

in the French Alps

Chet &
Carolee
Lipton

Printed in the United States of America

Gateway Books
Oakland, CA

Distributed by Publishers Group West

Library of Congress Cataloging-in-Publication Data

Lipton, Chet.
    Walking easy in the French Alps / Chet & Carolee Lipton.
        p.   cm.
    Includes index.
    ISBN 0-933469-21-7
        1. Hiking—France—French Alps—Guidebooks. 2. Trails—France—
French Alps, French—Guidebooks. 3. French Alps--Description and travel.
4. Walking--France--Paris--Guidebooks. 5. Paris (France)
-- Description. I. Lipton, Carolee. II. Title
GV199.44.F82F745 1995
796.5'1'09449—dc20   95-13325
                                                                          CIP

10 9 8 7 6 5 4 3 2 1

Acknowledgements:

The authors wish to thank the following for their assistance and guidance:

Marion Fourestier, Assistant Director of Public Relations, French Government Tourist Office; Air France; Kemwel Car Rental and Leasing, Harrison, New York; and the helpful staffs of Tourist Information Offices in Bourg-Saint-Maurice/Les Arcs, Chamonix/Mont Blanc, Embrun, Les Orres, Megève, Méribel, the Queyras, and the Rhône-Alpes.

A special *merci* to Mme. Claude Chowanietz, Director l'Embrunais Tourist Office; M. André Seigneur, Director Megève Tourist Office; M. Jean Marc Silva, Director Bourg-Saint-Maurice/Les Arcs Tourist Office; Ms. Françoise Daviet, Service Edition Méribel Tourist Office.

Another note of thanks goes to the hotel owners and staffs for providing the authors with local village history, general background information and helpful hints about their walking trails.

To Sue and Steve; Barbara, Arnie and Dustin—
the next generation of *Easy Walkers*.

CONTENTS

Becoming an *Easy Walker*   **11**

Timing Is Everything • Arriving in France by Airplane • France by Train • France by Car • France Up and Down • French Discount Travel • Comfortable Inns and Hotels • Enjoying French Cuisine • Where to Eat and Drink • Dressing for the Trail • Pack Light and Right • FYI: From Telephones to Tipping • Rules of the Road • Explanation of Symbols

PARIS •

FRANCE

Chamonix •
Megève
Bourg-St. Maurice/Les Arcs •
• Méribel

• Embrun

BECOMING AN EASY WALKER

Any seasoned traveler can cite compelling reasons to visit France for a romantic summer holiday. These inducements might include Paris' sensual, late-night entertainments, visits to the Louvre, dining at famous French restaurants, breathtaking vistas from the Eiffel Tower, or perhaps tours of the extraordinary medieval ramparts of Carcassonne, a slow stroll through the flower fields of Provence, or a ride as the fearless captain of a rented barge on one of France's scenic canals.

American tourists visit France for many reasons, but usually bypass what we consider to be one of the most romantic sojourns of them all: the French Alps. Take a moment and imagine the cool, crisp, clean alpine air, filled with the enticing fragrance of wildflowers; lush, green meadows framed by graceful, snow-capped peaks; the tantalizing aroma of country cooking wafting from the well-used, weathered brick chimneys of mountainside chalet restaurants and *refuges*.

The French Alps stretch from Lake Geneva to the Mediterranean Sea. Here are 230 miles (370 km) of mountain scenery embracing three national—Mercantour, Ecrins and Vanoise—and two regional—Vercors and Queyras—parks, all created to protect the splendid natural habitat of this tranquil region.

The walking trails in the French Alps match the beauty and natural quality of those in neighboring alpine countries. The trail system is supported by helpful local Tourist Offices and sincere, friendly villagers, anxious to share the wonders of their walking paths with day-walkers from around the world. *Walking Easy in the French Alps,* like its predecessors covering Italy, Austria and Switzerland, is a how-to book, devoted to each area's most beautiful walks that can be completed in one day by recreational walkers.

It is recommended that *Easy Walkers* spend at least one week in each location—Chamonix and Megève in the Haute-Savoie, Méribel and Bourg-St-Maurice/Les Arcs in the Savoie, and Embrun in the Hautes-Alpes—establishing a "base village" from where the walks can be reached. We use Paris as our gate of entry and departure in spite of the close proximity of the French Alps to Geneva, because we feel that a trip to France is not complete without a visit to Paris, one of the major cultural capitals of Europe. To that end, this guide also includes a section detailing a short walking tour of Paris, written especially for *Easy Walkers.*

Every walk in this guidebook is preceded by a description of its location, followed by directions to the start of the walk from the base village. Many walks begin with a mountain railway or cable car, while others are gentle walks through the forest or around a lake. Some are above the treeline or near a glacier, others descend through alpine meadows. Unless specifically mentioned, the paths are well-maintained and well-signed. Each walk is graded into one of three classifications: **Gentle**, low-level walks with few ascents and descents, through valleys and around lakes and rivers; **Comfortable**, ascents and descents over mixed terrain; and **More Challenging**, longer, more challenging ascents and descents on narrower trails. All walks can be accomplished in two to five hours by recreational walkers of any age in good health.

In addition to easy-guide maps of each walk, you will also find one or more recommended hiking maps listed at the beginning of each village's **Walks** section. These and other maps can be bought at the local Tourist Information office ("i") or newspaper/magazine stores. While the map is a necessity, you may also find it fun to carry a small, inexpensive compass to check directions and a pedometer to keep track of walking distances.

The walking time listed before each walk is time spent **actually** walking, **not** including breaks for lunch, resting, photography, sightseeing and transportation. This additional time is left to the discretion of each *Easy Walker* so that an average day with a three-hour walk usually begins at 9:00 or 10:00 am and ends back at the hotel by late afternoon.

The French Alps have hundreds of miles of trails, and as in our other guidebooks covering Switzerland, Austria and Italy, the paths in the French Alps were chosen for their beauty, walking time and ease of use. But, be warned—not all the hikes are easy. Many will joyously challenge your capabilities with ascents and descents over mixed terrain. However, it is not uncommon for people of all ages to be steadily wending their way along favorite trails—walking is not just for the young, it is also for the young at heart. The French have created a wonderful trail system, and it is the best way to see their magnificent countryside—walkers are welcome almost everywhere in their hiking boots and backpacks.

You can do it—just tuck a copy of *Walking Easy in the French Alps* in a pocket, and you are on your way!

Timing Is Everything

The French Alps are located south of Lake Geneva (Lac Léman), from the Haute-Savoie, south to the Savoie and to the Hautes-Alpes, and south again to the Alpes de Haute Provence and the Alpes Maritimes, bordering on the Mediterranean regions. However, the famous winter ski towns of France—and their summer walking trails—are concentrated in the northern alpine regions, the high mountains of the Haute-Savoie, the Savoie and the Hautes-Alpes.

Hiking season in the French Alps usually starts at the beginning of July and lasts through the early part of September. If you have a choice of selecting the timing of your walking vacation, there are fewer tourists and cooler temperatures in the beginning of July and in early September. These are ideal months for walking, with cloudless blue skies the norm, although by autumn the snow has melted from all except the highest mountain peaks and meadow flowers are dried pods, blowing in the fields. Mid-July and August, although warmer and busier, feature brilliant explosions of wildflowers throughout the meadows and valleys. While cities are crowded with European summer vacationers, remember that the serenity of shaded forests and high alpine trails is hardly ever shattered by too many walkers.

☞ **HINT: Lifts are an integral part of *Walking Easy* itineraries, and are usually in operation in the French Alps in July, August and the first week of September. When planning your walking holiday, make sure you confirm lift operating schedules with the local Tourist Office.**

Throughout the summer the riotous colors of alpine meadow flowers, framed against the mountain peaks, is breathtaking. The unusual color intensity of alpine blooms—the purple of crocus, daphne mezereum, mountain anemone and soldanella of the alps; the yellow of wild tulip and arnica; the white of pheasant's-eye; the blue of gentian and thistle; the pink of rose of the alps; the orange of the lily; and the dark red of the marshes orchid—comes from the greater intensity of the sun's strong ultraviolet rays at higher altitudes. In any month, *Walking Easy in the French Alps* can be exhilarating.

☞ HINT: High elevations can be quite cool in summer, especially in the early morning and evening. Keep an insulated jacket and rainwear (a good quality poncho) at the bottom of your backpack.

Arriving in France by Airplane

If you are flying into France for a walking vacation, many airlines offer non-stop flights to Paris, with a change of plane to other cities closer to the Alps—such as Geneva, Nice or Lyon. If you haven't visited Paris, this might be a good time to extend your alpine walking vacation. Air France offers direct flights to Paris from the following cities in the United States: Houston, Los Angeles, Miami, New York, San Francisco, and Washington, DC.

Geneva, Switzerland, is the closest large international airport to the French Alps, usually involving a change of plane from Paris or Zurich. Milan, Italy, is a possible alternative, especially if your first stop is Chamonix, easily accessible from Italy by driving via the Mont-Blanc Tunnel. From your point of arrival, options are available to villages in the Alps by rental car, train or bus. However, the fastest and most convenient means of transportation between the French alpine base villages is by automobile.

France by Train

The French National Railways (Société Nationale des Chemins de Fer or SNCF) is owned and operated by the French government. Included in this system are the TGV or high-speed Train à Grande Vitesse, EC (EuroCity), IC (Inter-City), Rapides or expresses, and car-carrying trains or TAC (Trains Autos-Couchettes). Only a few local railways are not part of this system.

☞ **HINT: Train cars are marked with a large "1" or "2" to denote class. For daytime travel, save by booking second class; it's almost as comfortable and clean as first class.**

Reservations are required for certain trains: selected EuroCity, InterCity and all TGV.

☞ **HINT: During July and August, reservations are advisable on ALL trains. In the United States, reservations can be made through Rail Europe, 1-800-438-7245. In France, make your reservations at train stations and SNCF offices.**

France by Car

If you are going to be in France for a walking vacation in the Alps, it will be more convenient to have an automobile at your disposal. A car gives Easy Walkers the opportunity of driving to the Alps from Paris on good roads through the lovely French countryside. United States citizens need a U.S. Driver's License to rent a car in France. An International Driver's Permit is recommended but not required. If you are going to leave France for another country in your rental car, inform the car rental agency staff in advance so proof of liability insurance can be checked. If you buy and use a car in France, you must have an International Insurance Certificate called a "green card."

☞ **HINT: In addition to helping you rent and drive in Europe, an International Driver's Permit is also useful for additional, easily understood identification (it's not mandatory) and can be obtained in the United States through AAA for $10 and two passport-size photos.**

In France, driving is on the right side of the road, the same as in the United States. Remember that a car coming from the right always has the right of way. Distances are measured in kilometers (1 kilometer = .62 miles). Speed is measured in kilometers per hour (kmph): 130 kmph (81 mph) is the speed limit on toll highways and expressways; 100 kmph (62 mph) on major highways; 90 kmph (56 mph) on country roads and 60 kmph (37 mph) through towns and villages. Large fines can be imposed for exceeding the speed limits. French law requires seat belts to be worn in both the front and back seats.

☞ **HINT: Many cities, including Paris, forbid the use of car horns—flash your lights instead.**

Most major highways (designated "A" on maps) are *autoroutes à péage* or toll roads. *Routes nationales* (N), are free roads and *routes départementales* (D) are secondary roads. Michelin driving map no.989 of France is a good choice for the entire country, but regional maps are also published for different areas, and you may want to purchase one for the alpine regions.

☞ **HINT: *Une panne* means "car breakdown," but if you dial 17, the police will give you the telephone number of a garage with towing facilities. On an expressway, use the emergency phone box for a direct connection to a facility that can help you.**

If you are going to be in Europe more than three weeks, it might be more economical to use a purchase-and-buy-back program. This involves the actual purchase of a new automobile, with a guaranteed buy-back at the end of a specified period of time. You will pay a set charge, and in France, this includes insurance in order to get the "green card" needed to drive in most European countries.

HINT: If you are interested in leasing a car, deal with a reliable company in the United States, completing all transactions at least 30 days before leaving the country. The purchase-and-buy-back program will save you the Value Added Tax (VAT) charged on rental cars. For example, KEMWEL, one of several international automobile rental/lease companies, has offices in Harrison, New York (telephone: 1-800-678-0678). The Kemwel Purchase and Buy Back Program is effective for any period from 14 to 175 days and includes a new Peugeot car and insurance, with delivery in many French locations. Make sure you check all insurance details, such as collision, theft, deductibles, etc.

France Up and Down

The following are important adjuncts to transportation in the French Alps.

Cable Cars (*téléphériques*) - These are large, enclosed cars holding up to 100 people, running on a fixed schedule. Example: the giant cable car from la Saulire peak above Méribel down to Courchevel.

Gondolas (*télécabines*) - They usually hold four to eight people, are enclosed, and run continuously. Example: the Transarc gondola from Les Arc 1800 above Bourg-Saint-Maurice.

Chairlifts (*télésièges*) - Sit-down lifts that move continuously and are usually open to the weather. They can be single, double or triple-chair systems. Example: the chairlift rising to the peak at Réallon, near Embrun.

Funiculars - Mountain railways pulled up and down a steep incline by a cable. Example: the funicular linking Bourg-St. Maurice to Arc 1600.

Cogwheel or **Rack and Pinion Railways** - These trains move by a toothed wheel connecting into the matching teeth of the rail. Example: the Mer de Glace mountain railway in Chamonix, winding its way up to one of Europe's largest glaciers.

> ☞ **HINT: In preparation for getting on the chairlift, remove your backpack and step on the platform. Sit down on the chair as it moves slowly under you, pulling down on the bar above, and rest your feet on the footrest. Just before entering the top station, as you glide onto the platform, take your feet off the footbar at the same time you raise the handle in front of you. Quickly step off the chair, following the arrows.**

French Discount Travel

While an automobile is the most convenient means of transportation in the French Alps, the following discount travel information is included for those who do not wish to drive. Please note that the prices of all passes are as of the 1994 season and are provided for comparison purposes only.

France Railpass	1st Class	2nd Class
any 3 days in 1 month	$175	$125
additional rail day (6 max.)	$ 39	$ 29

Travel any three days out of one month, consecutively or non-consecutively, with the option to purchase up to six extra days of rail travel.

France Rail 'n Drive Pass (Two Adults)

	1st Class	2nd Class	+Day Car
Cat. A - Economy	$195	$159	$ 39
Cat. B - Small	$225	$199	$ 55
Cat. C - Medium	$250	$219	$ 75
Cat. D - Small Automatic	$249	$199	$ 65
Additional rail day (6 max.)	$ 39	$ 29	

Travel any six days out of one month—three by rail, three by car. We recommend that you take the train for longer distances and use the rental car for side trips. Unlimited mileage car rentals are available in three categories of manual transmission and one category of automatic, with the option to purchase up to six extra travel days of rail and/or car rental, local tax included.

France Rail 'n Fly Pass

	1st Class	2nd Class
Any 4 days within 1 month	$269	$215
Additional rail day (6 maximum)	$ 39	$ 29
Additional rail trip	$ 85	$ 85

Travel any four days out of one month—three by rail, one by air. Air travel is with the French domestic airline Air Inter, for "M" Class on 5000 series flights only. Train days and air vouchers may be used consecutively or non-consecutively, with the option to purchase up to six extra rail travel days, as well as extra air travel vouchers which are each good for a one-way trip in France.

France Fly Rail 'n Drive Pass (Two Adults)

	1st Class	2nd Class	+Day Car
Cat. A - Economy	$279	$245	$ 39
Cat. B - Small	$309	$285	$ 55
Cat. C - Medium	$345	$305	$ 75
Cat. D - Small Automatic	$335	$285	$ 65
Additional Rail Day (6 max.)	$ 39	$ 29	
Additional Air Trip	$ 85	$ 85	

Travel any seven days out of one month—three by rail, three by car and one by air. Unlimited mileage car rentals are available in four different categories. Air travel is by the French domestic airline, Air Inter, for "M" class on 5000 series flights. There is also the option to purchase up to six extra travel days of rail, car rental, and/or extra air vouchers, local tax included.

 HINT: All French Passes include the following travel bonuses: free rail transfer from Orly or Charles de Gaulle Airports to Paris and return, reduced rates on Seine River cruises with "Bateaux Parisiens," 50% discount off the private rail line from Nice to Digne.

Senior citizen's discounts include the Carte Vermeil or silver-gilt card, which can be bought at any railway station in France, with proof of age, by men and women ages 60 and older.

1. Carte Vermeil Quatre Temps - Cost: 140 FF (about $25), allows four rail trips within a year at 50% discount.

2. Carte Vermeil Plein Temps - Cost: 250 FF (about $45), allows unlimited train travel within a year at 50% discount.

No train travel is allowed with either senior discount pass from noon Friday to noon Saturday and from 3:00 pm Sunday to noon Monday. Reduced prices on certain local bus lines are available, as are 50% discounts on entrance fees to state-owned museums, and 25 to 50% discounts on Air Inter's regular, full fares.

Buy all passes (except senior discount) from your travel agent or Rail Europe, Inc. (1-800-4-EURAIL) **before** leaving for France. Additional travel days **must** be bought at the same time to qualify for the special rates. **Do not write on or fill in any part of your pass before it has been validated!**

Have your pass validated before your first French train ride, car rental or Air Inter flight by presenting your pass and passport to the railway official at the ticket window in the train station (not the conductor), who will enter the first and last date of your travel period. This should be done prior to your first train journey. After the pass is validated, before boarding the train each day the pass is used, write the date in ink on the pass in the correct box.

When you rent your car in France, present the pass and one car voucher for each rental day. Reserve your car rental at least seven days before your departure and confirm drop-off conditions at 1-800-331-1084.

Exchange your Air Inter voucher at the airport for your airplane ticket before boarding the plane. To make air reservations in the U.S. with Air Inter, call 1-800-237-2747 and request "M" Class on 5000 series flights.

Comfortable Inns and Hotels

Winter is more expensive than summer in alpine ski resorts such as Chamonix and Megève. Ski villages have built hotel and apartment accommodations to handle the winter sports enthusiasts, and since they are not always filled in spring, summer and autumn, rates can be lower. However, advance reservations are advisable in August when all of Europe seems to be on vacation. However, in Embrun, in the Hautes-Alpes near Lake Serre-Ponçon, summer is high season because of its proximity to the lake and its myriad of water sports.

Accommodations in France range from world-class, deluxe hotels to comfortable rooms in rural farmhouses. The quality of a hotel (and its prices), can be judged by the number of stars it is awarded. In France, **** **L** is equivalent to five-star deluxe in other European countries, **** is equivalent to first-class, *** indicates a superior, good quality tourist hotel, ** is a standard budget hotel, and * is a budget hotel, meeting minimum standards. Many bedrooms in one- or two-star hotels do not have private bathrooms, but contain hot and cold water and a bidet, or *cabinet de toilette*, while others may have only a sink.

We usually recommend three-star hotels, with demi-pension (half-board: breakfast and dinner), for comfort, quality of food, and overall value. If you prefer to dine at different restaurants each evening—more expensive (but not necessarily better) than dinner at your hotel on the half-board plan—try a hotel *garni*, a hotel that serves breakfast only and which is rated on the same star system as full-service hotels.

 HINT: When making hotel reservations, specify twin-bedded room for two with private bathroom facilities (if you desire a bathtub in addition to a shower, mention this) and demi-pension.

Furnished chalets and rental apartments are a viable alternative to hotels. The local Tourist Office in each French village can provide lists of places to rent. Write to the Tourist Office (Office du Tourisme) and then contact the home or apartment owner directly by airmail.

Fédération Nationale des Logis et Auberges de France, or **Logis de France**, is an association of over 4000, primarily one- and two-star, family-run, country inns and hotels combining economy with comfort and cleanliness, located throughout France. A **Logis en Liberté** program is available for purchase through your travel agent or Rail Europe before leaving the United States. Call Rail Europe to determine which categories of hotels are available in each location you plan to visit. Reserve the first hotel night, or all hotel nights, and purchase vouchers before leaving the country. For each overnight accommodation purchased you will receive one voucher per person. On checking into the hotel, present one voucher for each night you plan to stay.

If you are not planning a fixed itinerary, reserve the first night and then reserve from hotel to hotel as you travel. The cost for a hotel room for two persons in 1994 was $64 per night for the "Comfort" category, comfortable, tourist-class (two-star) inns, or $88 per night for "Comfort Plus" category, inns and lodges in scenic settings, some with swimming pools or saunas, and bedrooms with TV and telephones. Unused vouchers are refundable.

☞ **HINT:** In the Logis de France guide, hotels are graded by one, two or three fireplaces, based on 150 different criteria ranging from the quality of food and service to the standard of the room and general facilities.

Bed-and-breakfast accommodations are called *gîtes-chambres d'hôte* in France. Write **La Maison du Tourisme Vert Fédération Nationale des Gîtes Ruraux-de-France**, 35, rue Godet-de-Mauroy, 75009 Paris, for a list of over 6000 accommodations, ranging from simple farmhouses to luxurious castles. If you are interested in bed-and-breakfast stays in France, two books are particularly useful. ***French Country Welcome* (1994)** lists thousands of *chambre d'hôte* members of the Gites de France organization. It is written in English and can be found in some tourist offices in France. ***Guides des Maison d'Hôtes de Charme en France***, describing over three hundred B&Bs, is written in French with easily understood basic descriptions. It can be bought from the Librairie de France in New York city (tel: 212-265-1094) and is available in France at many bookstores.

Formule 1 hotels are very basic and strictly budget, with rooms costing about $25 per night, usually in the outlying areas of cities. They accept charge cards. For a free copy of their list of hotels, write to: Chaîne des Hôtels Formule 1, B.P. 159, 93163 Noisy-le-Grand, France.

Other budget travelers may find the **Campanile** hotels, about 300 two-star, family-run hotels around France, a viable alternative to any of the above. They also work on a prepaid voucher program and provide buffet breakfast for an extra 30 FF per person. Contact Hometours International, Inc., 800-367-4668, for more information.

☞ HINT: Prices quoted by hotels include taxes, tips and breakfast, unless otherwise noted.

Many small hotels do not require a deposit; if you write or fax them directly they will confirm the cost of your room and food arrangements, dates of arrival and departure with a welcoming letter. Remember, a complete listing and information about hotels can be obtained by writing directly to the local Tourist Information Office in each city, town and village.

☞ HINT: Many smaller hotels in rural or mountain areas do not accept credit cards. Check with your hotel, and if this is the case, make sure you bring enough traveler's checks to cover all your bills, as they do not accept personal checks drawn on United States banks.

Enjoying French Cuisine

Most French meals consist of several courses: the *hors d'oeuvre* (appetizer) or *potage* (soup), a meat course with vegetables, salad (usually following the main course unless requested otherwise), a cheese tray, and dessert.

Cheese - The cheeses of alpine Savoie are varied in shape, color and taste. Reblochon, produced more than other area cheeses, is made from the whole, crude milk of local cows, maturing in a cold cellar in only three to four weeks. Beaufort is called "the prince of Gruyères," a creamy cheese made in the traditional manner. Emmental with its holes, smooth, shiny surface and fruity taste is made in the foothills of the Savoie and Haute-Savoie and needs about ten weeks to reach maturity. Tomme de Savoie is the oldest of the Savoie and Haute-Savoie cheeses. Tomme des Bauges is made with crude milk only in the Massif des Bauges region in the heart of the Savoie alps—it has a fruity taste with a coarse rind after maturing for forty days in humid cellars. Made in the mountains of the Haute-Savoie, the Chevrotin des Aravis is a farmhouse cheese produced from goat's milk. Made since the 14th century, Abondance is from the milk of local cows in mountain chalets in summer and in dairies in winter. Tamié is made with whole, crude cow's milk, produced exclusively in the mountains by Trappist monks from the Abbey of Tamié near Albertville; look for its unique packaging, a white Maltese cross on a blue background.

A French Food Primer

aïoli - mayonnaise with garlic
assiette du pêcher - mixed seafood platter
baguette - loaf of bread
béarnaise - sauce made with egg yolks, shallots, white wine, vinegar, butter and tarragon
béchamel - sauce made with butter, flour, onions and herbs
blanquette - meat stew with a white sauce
boeuf à la mode - marinated beef stew made with red wine and vegetables
boeuf en daube - beef stew with red wine
bouillabaisse - Mediterranean fish soup
bourguigonon - Burgandy-style, i.e., with red wine, bacon and onions
carré d'agneau - roast lamb
confit - usually duck or goose, cooked and preserved in its own fat
coq au vin - chicken stew with red wine and mushrooms
côte d'agneau - lamb chop
côte de boeuf - rib steak
crème brûlée - custard dessert with caramelized topping
crème chantilly - sweet whipped cream
crème fraîche - sour, heavy cream
croque-monsieur - toasted sandwich containing ham and cheese
farci - stuffed
fraise des bois - wild strawberries
fricassée - braised meat or poultry
gelée - jelly or aspic
gâteau - cake
glaces - ice cream

gratin - dish with crust of bread crumbs and melted cheese
grenouilles - frog's legs
hollandaise - sauce with egg yolks, butter and lemon juice
huile d'olive - olive oil
jardinière - garnish of freshly cooked vegetables
legume - vegetable
limande - lemon sole
lotte - monkfish
loup de mer - Mediterranean sea bass
macédoine - mixture of fruits
marmite - thick vegetable and beef soup
meunière - rolled in flour and sautéed in butter
millefeuille - a napoleon
mornay - béchamel sauce with cheese
oeufs à la neige - egg whites poached in milk and served on custard
pain - bread
pamplemouse - grapefruit
parfait - layered ice cream
pâté - ground meat or vegetables, baked in a mold
poisson - fish
pomme - apple
pommes frites - french fries
porc - pork
pot au feu - stew cooked in an earthenware pot
poulet - chicken
profiteroles - small cream puffs
ragoût - beef stew
ris de veau - veal sweetbreads
rôti - roasted
sabayon - egg custard with marsala wine
salade niçoise - salad with tomatoes, string beans, tuna, black
  olives, potatoes, artichokes and capers
sommelier - wine steward
sorbet - fruit sherbet
soufflé - airy, baked, egg dish
steak au poivre - flambéed steak covered with peppercorns
suprême - white sauce made with heavy cream
tartare - cold, chopped raw meat
tarte tatin - caramelized upside-down apple tart
vacherin - ice cream in a meringue shell
véronique - garnished with grapes
vichyssoise - cold potato and leek soup
vol-au-vent - puff pastry shell

Beverages

Wine - Taste the wines of the Savoie Alps: the ancient vineyards from Lake Geneva south to below Chambéry overlook rivers and lakes on alpine slopes and flourish in the pure mountain air. The white wines are fruity and dry, best served cool with local fish, or fondue and raclette (a Swiss specialty featuring heated, shaved cheese). The red and rosé wines of the Savoie, light and fragrant, compliment regional dishes and local cheeses. The sparkling wines have an excellent reputation.

> ☞ **HINT: Drinking unlabeled house wine in bottles or carafes—*vin de la maison*—is less expensive and is also enjoyable. The French usually spend a third of their restaurant bill on wine.**

If you are interested in setting up an appointment to taste the area wines, write to Comité Interprofessionnal des Vins de Savoie, 3 rue du Château, 7300 Chambéry, France, for a list of wine producers, bottling firms, cooperative wineries and wine merchants in the Savoie. You can drive through the vineyards of the Savoie Alps through pleasant backroads by following the "Route of Wines."

One trip is in the direction of la Combe de Savoie: Chambéry, les Charmettes, St-Baldolph, Myans, Apremont, St-André, les Marches, Chapareillan, Montmélian, Arbin, Cruet, St-Jean de la Porte, St-Pierre d'Albigny, Fréterive. Return by main roads RN 90 and 6 up to Montmélian, Chignin, St-Jeoire Prieuré, Challes-les-Eaux, Barby, St-Alban-Leysse to Chambéry.

Another route is around the Lake of Bourget: Chambéry, Aix-les-Bains, Brison-St-Innocent, Chindrieux, Ruffieux, Serrières-en-Chautagne, Motz, Seyssel, Frangy, then return by Chindrieux, Chaudieu, and go around the lake by St-

Pierre de Curtille, the Abbey of Hautecombe, Lucey, Jongieux, Billième, Monthoux, the Tunnel du Chat, le Bourget du Lac and Chambéry.

Liqueur - After-dinner liqueurs such as Marc or Armagnac, called *digestif*, are supposed to aid in the digestive processes. Brandy, distilled from fruits or herbs, such as Eau-de-Vie ("Water of Life"), has a very high alcohol content and is also drunk at the end of the meal. Marc and Brulôt Savoyard are traditional brandies.

> ☞ **HINT: An *apéritif* before dinner supposedly awakens the appetite. It is also less expensive than scotch, vodka, or other such liquors.**

Mineral Water - Bottled mineral water, with or without "gas," is available everywhere.

Where to Eat and Drink

Hotels: Three-star French alpine hotels usually offer a continental breakfast consisting of orange juice, hot beverage, a basket of rolls/bread and croissants, butter and preserves. If you reserve a room with demi-pension (half-board), dinner can be a soup and/or appetizer, main course with potatoes and vegetables, cheese and/or dessert. (If desired, fresh fruit can usually be substituted for the dessert.) Coffee, tea or hot chocolate are included with breakfast but always cost extra at dinner. Hotel food in France is uniformly excellent and *Easy Walkers* can take advantage of lower costs by booking demi-pension.

> ☞ **HINT: Most diners prefer to take their after-dinner coffee later in the evening at an outdoor café or hotel sitting room.**

Restaurants: If you decide to eat in a restaurant outside your hotel, notify the hotel desk 24 hours in advance so the day's demi-pension charge can be deducted from your bill. In a restaurant, *plat du jour* means the daily special, while *table d'hôte* is a price-fixed, pre-selected meal, usually offering no choice of specific dishes that comprise it. Less expensive restaurants may include a beverage in the menu price, called *boisson compris.* A 15% service charge (tip) is *always* included in your bill. A few small coins should be left on the table if you were pleased with the service.

> ☞ **HINT: It is polite to refer to your waiter as *monsieur*, not *garcon*.**

Picnicking: When planning a day of walking, we recommend taking a picnic lunch in your backpack. Fresh bread or rolls can be bought at the local bakery (*boulangerie*). Select a local cheese and/or sliced cooked meat in the delicatessen (*charcuterie*) or butcher shop (*boucherie*). Fresh fruit completes a healthy and inexpensive meal. Mustard can be bought in reusable squeeze tubes. Mineral water, juice and soda are available in plastic bottles or cans at the grocery store (*épicerie*).

Dressing for the Trail—From Boots to Backpack

Walking Easy clothing should ideally be lightweight and layerable. All clothing is not suitable for all types of walking—climate, altitude and time of day during the alpine hiking season are points to consider. *Easy Walkers* must make the decision each day, taking the above factors into consideration. Note that small villages may not have laundry facilities or hotel valet service (which can be expensive), so if you wash underwear, socks and knit shirts EVERY night before dinner, you will always be ahead of the washing game. Remember that clothes can take longer to dry if they are 100% cotton. Shirts or underwear containing poly/cotton will dry overnight.

☞ **HINT: On your first day in France, buy a 250 ml tube of *Genie - gel express a la main* (in a bright blue tube with white lettering), eliminating the need to carry detergent from home.**

Shoes: The most important item in a successful walking holiday is a good pair of broken-in, light to medium-weight hiking boots, preferably waterproof. These can be above or below the ankle, with the higher ones providing more support on rocky or steep trails. Do **not** wear sneakers or sneakers that look like hiking boots; they do not provide the support and traction needed. Remember, $60 hiking boots do not have the same level of construction as $120 boots— the durability, waterproofing, foot stability and overall quality are not the same in a less expensive shoe. All boots will probably feel good when the trail is wide, level and smooth, but remember the ascents, descents, stones and rain!

Socks: When purchasing good quality hiking boots, wear the combination of socks you will use for walking. Experts tell us that socks worn closest to the skin should **not** be made of cotton. Cotton absorbs perspiration and holds it, possibly producing friction, leading to blisters. A lightweight under-sock made of a "hydrophobic" or water-hating synthetic will wick sweat away from your feet and keep them drier. Whether you prefer to wear one or two pair of socks, when purchasing hiking boots, make sure you wear the combination you will wear on the trail.

☞ **HINT: Eliminate your heaviest packable item by wearing your hiking boots on the airplane and whenever traveling.**

Outer Clothing: An insulated jacket or vest is essential for walking and for sightseeing over 8000 ft. (2500 m). These jackets are easily put into backpacks when not needed and can be carried on the plane. Rain protection is best provided by a good quality waterproof poncho, with a snap-down back to fit over a backpack (such as is available from L.L.Bean), or waterproof long pants and jacket. Don't let a drizzle or light rain cancel your walking plans.

> ☞ **HINT: Rain gear should always be stowed at the bottom of your backpack until needed.**

Hats: A hat with a brim provides protection from sun as well as rain and **should be worn at all times.**

Pants: Many alpine walkers wear blue jeans—a good choice if they are not tight and/or heavy and do not restrict movement. Cotton chinos are also satisfactory, and in summer, walking shorts should definitely be considered. However, our favorite walking apparel in any type of climate is alpine hiking knickers. They fasten below the knee and are worn with high socks that protect the legs from bushes and brambles, cold temperatures and insects, but which can be rolled down in warmer weather. These knickers, for both men and women, are comfortable for all types of walking, and you'll see them being worn on trails all over Europe. They can be purchased in most French sporting goods stores.

Sweaters: Medium-weight sweaters are essential for cool evenings in the mountains, even in summer.

Sweatshirts: Medium-weight sweatshirts can be layered over short- or long-sleeved knits for hiking.

Shirts: While many people prefer 100% natural fibers for comfort in shirts, a cotton/polyster blend can be used for ease of laundering, as they will dry overnight. Short-sleeved knit shirts, along with turtlenecks and long-sleeved shirts, are essential for layering under sweaters or sweatshirts, both day and evening.

> ☞ **HINT: It is not necessary to bring a dress, skirt, sport jacket, stockings, dress shoes or pocketbook on this walking vacation. However, a classic mix of slacks layered with shirts and sweaters is essential and can take you to dinner or sightseeing. In fact, the mix and match possibilities of two pair of slacks, two knit turtlenecks, two long-sleeved blouses/shirts and two sweaters have taken the authors through two months of alpine evenings!**

Backpack: Every *Easy Walker* should carry a lightweight nylon backpack with wide, extra-heavy, adjustable foam shoulder straps. Roomy, outside zipper compartments are necessary to organize backpacking essentials, i.e., camera equipment, lunch, water, sunscreen, binoculars, emergency roll of toilet paper, rain gear, jacket or sweater, etc.

Waist or Fanny Pack: Use a well-made, comfortable waist pack to carry money, travelers checks, passport, etc. No pocketbook or purse is necessary on a walking vacation. Hands should be left free for walking sticks and cameras.

Walking Stick: We recommend a walking cane or walking stick with a pointed, metal tip for all *Easy Walkers*. These sticks are an indispensible aid to balance when walking downhill or on rocky terrain. They come in many sizes and styles and can usually be purchased at any French village sporting goods store.

> ☞ **HINT: The newest walking stick innovation looks like a telescoping aluminum ski pole and fits into a backpack when not in use.**

Luggage Carrier: A small, fold-up luggage carrier can be useful to transport luggage from the train or bus station, or even your car, to the hotel. Even easier to use is the new, lightweight luggage with built in wheels and handle.

Pack Light and Right

Keep luggage small, lightweight and expandable, even when using a luggage carrier or traveling by car.

1. Wear your hiking boots for overseas and inter-village travel—they can be bulky to pack. Remove them on the plane, perhaps changing to a pair of lightweight slippers you have put into your backpack.

2. On the airplane, wear comfortable slacks, a knit shirt, and an unlined jacket, along with your waist pack and hiking boots. A lightweight warm-up suit can be a good alternative—the jacket can be worn as a windbreaker when it is too warm for your insulated jacket.

3. Every *Easy Walker* should have a lightweight backpack to use as carry-on luggage. When traveling, your backpack should include:

   a) All drugs and toiletries, with prescriptions in a separate, zippered pouch for easy accessibility.
   b) For the plane: one change of socks, underwear and knit shirt, rolled into a plastic bag—just in case.
   c) Slippers for plane and bedroom use.
   d) Insulated jacket (you might want to carry this).
   e) Waterproof outerwear.
   f) Roll of emergency toilet paper in a plastic bag.
   g) Reading material.
   h) Incidentals such as: binoculars, compass, pedometer, whistle, tiny flashlight, pocket knife, plastic bags, small sewing kit, sunglasses, travel alarm, address

book or pre-printed mailing labels, small packs of tissues and "handi-wipes," and of course, your *Walking Easy* guide-book.

i) Photographic equipment, unless carried separately.

☞ **HINT: If you wear glasses, pack a spare pair along with a copy of your prescription.**

EASY WALKER UNISEX PACKING CHECKLIST

_____ 6 pr. underpants
_____ 3 bras
_____ 7 pr. socks (3 long hiking, 2 undersocks, 2 evening)
_____ 2 pr. shoes (1 hiking, 1 evening)
_____ 1 pr. slippers
_____ 1 belt
_____ 1 pajamas/nightgown
_____ 1 lightweight robe (optional)
_____ 1 bathing suit (optional)
_____ 2 sweaters
_____ 2 sweatshirts
_____ 1 insulated jacket or vest
_____ 1 lightweight outer jacket
_____ 2 pr. hiking pants or knickers
_____ 2 pr. casual slacks
_____ 1 or 2 pr. walking shorts
_____ 2 shirts or blouses, long-sleeved
_____ 4 knit shirts, short-sleeved
_____ 2 knit shirts, long-sleeved turtleneck
_____ 1 hat
_____ 1 rain outfit, poncho

For Your Information—From Telephones to Tipping

Credit Cards: Most retail stores accept credit cards, as do hotels and restaurants. Mountains inns (*refuges*) however, do not. In France, MasterCard may be called Eurocard and Visa can be known as Carte Bleu. Both are widely accepted, along with American Express and Diners Club. Charging can work in your favor because of the better rate of exchange large companies receive.

☞   **HINT: Keep a record of charge card numbers and the telephone numbers for reporting a lost or stolen card in a separate place from where you keep your credit cards.**

Customs: Returning from France to the United States, American citizens may bring back $400 in duty-free items if they've been outside the United States for at least 48 hours and not claimed exemptions in the previous 30 days. A flat rate of 10% is assessed for items valued at over $400. However, antiques at least 100 years old and paintings and drawings done by hand are duty-free. Gifts up to a total of $50 per day can be mailed home without declaring them on your customs form.

☞   **HINT: Keep all receipts of purchases in one place (we use a zip-lock plastic bag) where they can be easily retrieved.**

Documents: A valid passport is necessary for every traveler entering France. A visa is needed for longer stays than 90 days—apply to the French Embassy, 4001 Consulate Road NW, Washington, DC, 20007, tel: 202-944-6015, or the French Consulate at 935 Fifth Avenue, New York, NY, 10021, tel: 212-606-3653. **You must carry your passport or other proof of identification at all times in France.** While in France, if your passport is lost, contact the nearest United States consulate—they will issue you a temporary three-month passport. There are consulates in Paris, Bordeaux, Lyon, Marseilles, and Strasbourg.

☞   **HINT: Before leaving the United States, photocopy the information on your front passport pages in case it is** lost. Since you'll be carrying the original passport in your waist pack, put the copy in another location.

Electricity: France uses 220 or 230 volt, 50 cycle alternating current. Bring a converter and a plug adaptor because of different plug configurations in different areas.

Gasoline (*Essence*): There are many more self-service gasoline pumps in France than a few years ago, but gasoline is still very expensive. Leaded, unleaded and diesel gasolines are available, sold in liters (1 gallon = 3.7 liters). Most rental cars require unleaded gasoline (*sans plomb*).

> ☞ **HINT: Gas stations in rural areas of France may be hard to find unless you are driving on a toll highway, so top off your tank when it registers half-empty.**

Government: France is a republic, its Parliament divided into the National Assembly and the Senate, with the National Assembly enacting laws. The President is elected by majority for seven years, and he/she can only be elected twice in total.

Health: If you need a doctor in France, the hotel owner can help you. If you are in a small village, be prepared to travel to a larger town or city for specialized care. When you see a doctor, the fee is paid after his consultation. Make sure you receive a bill marked "paid," and contact your own health insurance company for reimbursement when you return home. A list of English-speaking doctors in France is available from the International Association for Medical Assistance to Travelers (AMAT) at 716-754-4883.

> ☞ **HINT: For a chronic illness such as diabetes or a heart condition, wear a Medic Alert Identification Tag. Call 800-432-5378 for information. This service also provides a 24-hour hotline a foreign doctor can call to access your medical records.**

Holidays: Banks, offices, stores, museums, monuments, and even many gas stations are closed on the following National Holidays:

Jan. 1	New Year's Day
varies	Shrove Tuesday (the Tuesday before Ash Wednesday)
varies	Good Friday
varies	Easter Sunday
varies	Easter Monday
May 1	Labor Day
May 8	V-E Day
varies	Ascension Day (40 days after Easter)
varies	Pentecost Sunday (seventh Sunday after Easter)
varies	Pentecost Monday
July 14	Bastille Day
Aug 15	Assumption of the Blessed Virgin
Nov. 1	All Saint's Day
Nov. 11	Armistice Day
Dec. 25	Christmas Day

Insurance: Before purchasing additional insurance of any kind, *Easy Walkers* should review their existing policies and determine whether coverage is adequate for overseas travel. Homeowner policies may cover luggage, theft and/or plane tickets—your insurance agent will tell you if you are covered.

> ☞ **HINT: Medicare provides emergency medical coverage for United States travelers to Mexico and Canada only. Check your Medicare supplement for overseas coverage.**

Contact your travel agent for companies offering the following types of travel insurance:

1) Trip cancellation and interruption - provides a refund if a trip must be cancelled or interrupted while in progress.

2) Personal accident and sickness - covers illness, injury or death.

3) Default and/or bankruptcy - coverage in case the airline, etc. defaults or goes bankrupt.

4) Baggage and personal effects - protects your luggage and contents against damage or theft.
5) Automobile insurance - for collision, theft, property damage, personal liability protection (check with your own insurance agent and your credit card company for these).

☞ **HINT: If you are driving in Europe you need an international insurance certificate, called a green card (*carte verte*). Your car rental agency MUST give you one before you take the car and begin your trip.**

Language: Following are translations of common French words found on directions and hiking maps.

arrêt - stop
attention - caution
barrage - dam
bois - wood
côte à forte inclination - steep incline
cul-de-sac - dead end
défense d'entrer - do not enter
défense de stationner - no parking
déviation - detour
droite - right
école - school
église - church
l'est - east
étang - pond
falaise - cliff
forêt - forest
gare - railway station
gauche - left

gorges - gorge
hôtel - mansion
jardin - garden
loin - far
mont - mount
musée - museum
le nord - north
l'ouest - west
péage - pay toll
pont - bridge
proche - near
ralentissez - reduce speed
rocher - rock
sens unique - one way
le sud - south
tour - tower
vallée - valley

The origins of the French language are in the intertwinings of the "dead" languages of Latin and Celtic. Two main language splits developed in the early Middle Ages: the *langue d'Oil* of Paris and the north, and *langue d'Oc* of the south. The northern language finally reigned supreme, but some ancient dialects can still be heard in remote provinces.

Until the end of World War II, Provençal was spoken in the south, Celtic Breton in the north, baffling Basque in the southwest, Catalán along sections of the border with Spain, German in Alsace and Lorraine, and a type of Flemish on the Belgian border.

Laundry: In larger towns, look in the telephone directory under *laverie automatic* for a coin-operated laundromat.

Mail: The Post Office, or Postes, Télécommunications, and Télédiffusion, is indicated on signs by "P et T." They are usually open from 8:00 am to 7:00 pm weekdays and 8:00 am to noon on Saturday. Letter boxes in France are painted bright yellow. All letters going overseas should be sent by airmail for faster delivery.

Mail from home can be forwarded to a French Post Office for collection. The envelope must have a return name and address, the name of the person who will collect the mail, the words *poste restante,* plus the name of the town preceded by the postal code and the country.

For example:
Mr. Artur Shambon
Poste Restante
74400 Chamonix, France

☞ **HINT: Stamps can be bought at tobacco shops (*tabacs*), hotel desks and some newstands as well as the post office.**

Medications: If you are taking a prescription drug, bring more than just an adequate supply, plus a prescription for the drug using its generic name in case it is neccesary for a local doctor to write a new prescription. Also, carry familiar, over-the-counter medications to counteract diarrhea, sunburn, constipation, indigestion, cuts and bruises, colds, allergies, etc. Put together a small first aid kit to carry in your backpack while walking—bandaids, antibiotic cream, aspirin, allergy pills—and of course, an effective sunscreen.

> ☞ **HINT: When traveling between villages, always carry medications in your backpack in case there is a problem with checked luggage.**

Metric System: France operates on the metric system. To change meters to feet, multiply meters by 3.281, and to convert kilometers to miles, multiply the number of kilometers by .62. To convert liters to quarts, multiply by .88, and to convert liters to US gallons, multiply the number of liters by .26. From grams to ounces, multiply grams by .035, and to convert kilograms to pounds, multiply the number of kilograms by 2.2. To convert Celsius to Fahrenheit degrees, multiply Celsius degrees by 9, divide by 5, and add 32.

Money: The basic unit of currency in France is the French Franc (FF), composed of 100 centimes. Paper bank notes are in 20, 50, 100, 200 and 500 FF denominations. Coins are 1, 2, 5, and 10 FF pieces and 5, 10, 20 and 50 centimes. The French use a comma where Americans use a decimal point, i.e. 21,50 is equivalent to 21 francs, 50 centimes.

The exchange rate fluctuates constantly, but to convert French francs to U.S. dollars, multiply the number of francs by the exchange rate. For example, if your hotel room costs 500 FF per day and the exchange rate is 1 FF = .18 $US, multiply 500 by .18—your hotel room will cost $90.

> ☞ **HINT: Money can be changed at all airports and railroad stations, as well as many banks. Expect to pay a commission on each transaction.**

Museums: As a rule, national museums are closed on Tuesdays, and city or municipal museums are closed on Mondays. Travelers over 60 years of age receive 50% discount to state museums with a Carte Vermeil.

Newspapers: Even in small towns, a store can usually be found that sells the *International Herald Tribune*, published in English Monday through Saturday, and/or the European edition of *U.S.A. Today*. Newsstands, or *kiosks* are also found at railroad stations. In smaller villages, these newspapers may arrive one day late, i.e., the Thursday paper is sold on Friday.

Restrooms: When no public restroom is available, you can use the lavatory in a café, but it is customary to make a small purchase if you do so, such as a cup of coffee.

Shopping Hours: Department and larger stores are usually open from 9:30 am to 6:30 pm, Monday to Saturday and remain open one day a week until 9:00 pm. Smaller stores are usually open Tuesday to Saturday from 10:00 am to noon and 2:00 pm to 6:30 pm. Small food stores can be open from 9:00 am to 12:30 pm and 3:30 pm to 7:00 pm. Check the shopping hours in each village—store closings vary considerably.

> ☞ **HINT: Proper French etiquette suggests the following when entering a store—nod and say *monsieur* or *madame* as greeting.**

Smoking: By French law, smoking is restricted in enclosed public places, including the Métro and its stations. Trains have designated smoking and non-smoking cars, and smoking is not allowed in the restaurant car. Smoking areas in hotels, restaurants and theaters are up to the discretion of management.

> ☞ **HINT: A smoking area is designated by *espace fumeur* and non-smoking is *espace non-fumeur*. On trains, smoking is designated by a cigarette, non-smoking by a cigarette with a red line through it.**

Telephones: When in France, use public phone booths instead of hotel phones because of the high service charges that will be added to your bill. Public phones are usually located in post offices, train stations, and cafés.

The minimum phone charge is 1 FF and pay phones accept 1, 2 and 5 franc coins or *jetons*, tokens bought at the Post Office, tobacco stores (*tabacs*), or cashiers at cafés.

To use a coin-operated public phone:
1. Pick up the phone receiver.
2. Insert the coin or *jeton*.
3. Dial when you hear the tone.
4. Push the button if someone answers.

Many public telephones in France accept only a plastic phone card called *télécartes*, bought at post offices, transportation centers, newsstands and tobacco stores.

To dial from a phone using a *télécarte*, follow the instructions on the screen as follows:
1. *Décrocher* - Pick up the receiver.
2. *Introduire carte ou fair numéro libre* - Insert the card and follow instructions.
3. *Fermer le volet SVP* - Close flap.
4. *Solde:x unités* - Number of calls remaining on card.
5. *Numérator* - Dial number.
6. *Numéro appelé* - The number you dialed appears on the screen.
7. *Retirer carte* - After you hang up, the flap opens automatically so you can take your card.

Some helpful telephone numbers to carry with you:
local information and operator - 12
ambulance - 15
police - 17
fire department - 18
international operator - 19

To be connected to United States phone company operators dial "19," wait for the tone, then dial "0011" for AT&T, "0019" for MCI, or "0087" for Sprint.

To make a station-to-station call from France to the United States dial 19, wait for a dial tone, then dial 1+area code+local number.

To call within the Paris/Ile-de-France area dial the local 8-digit number.

To call from Paris/Ile-de-France to the provinces dial 16, wait for a dial tone, then dial the 8-digit number.

To call from the provinces to Paris/Ile-de-France dial 16, wait for the dial tone, then dial 1+local 8-digit number.

To call between provinces dial the local 8-digit number.

☞ **HINT: If you telephone someone in France, the response may be *J'écoute* (pronounced "jay-coot"), literally "I hear."**

Time: France is six hours ahead of Eastern Standard Time in the United States. They use European Time, based on the 24-hour clock (i.e., 13:10 is 1:10 pm U.S.), and all timetables are written in this manner. Most of Europe converts to daylight savings time from the last Sunday in March to the last Sunday in September.

Tipping: By law, all restaurant bills have a 15% service charge or *servis compris* built into the cost. It is customary, however, to leave some small coins on the table, or another 10 FF, if you enjoyed the service. Taxi drivers are usually tipped 10% to 15% of the meter, porters 10 FF per bag, restroom attendants 2 FF, ushers 2 FF, and hairdressers 10% of the bill.

Tourist Information Offices: The Office du Tourisme, designated in France by a sign with an "i," is a valuable friend to the hiker. You will usually find Tourist Offices on the main street in even the smallest communities, near or in the railroad station in larger towns. The personnel are friendly and multilingual and can help with everything from hotel reservations to local hiking maps. When preparing for your trip write to the Office du Tourisme in the towns you intend visiting, and ask them to send information on hotels and walking and sightseeing activities.

The French Government Tourist Offices can provide information on accommodations, sightseeing, and general information about every aspect of a vacation in France. They accept telephone inquiries at 1-900-990-0040, at a cost of $.50 per minute. Write to them at the following locations:

9454 Wilshire Blvd., Suite 303, Beverly Hills, CA 90212
645 N. Michigan Ave., Suite 630, Chicago, IL 60611
2305 Cedar Springs Rd., Suite 205, Dallas, TX 75201
610 Fifth Ave., New York, NY 10020
(walk-in information office: 628 Fifth Ave., New York)

Traveler's Checks: Before leaving home you can purchase American traveler's checks, but when you convert them into French francs you'll pay a commission. To avoid the service charge and the waiting lines, buy traveler's checks in French franc denominations. Most large banks and the AAA offer this service to their customers—you'll pay the exchange rate of the day of purchase. They are easily converted to cash or used as cash with no extra charge in France.

United States Embassy and Consulates:

Embassy:
2, av. Gabriel, Paris 75008, tel: 1-42-96-12-02
Passports are reissued at 2, rue St-Florentin, tel: 1-42-96-12-02, ext. 2613.

Consulates:
22, cours du Maréchal-Foch, 33080 Bordeaux, tel: 56-52-65-95
12, bd. Paul Peytral, 13286 Marseilles, tel: 91-54-92-00
15, av. d'Alsace, 67082 Strasbourg, tel: 88-35-31-04

Value Added Tax (VAT): A Taxe à la Valeur Ajoutée or **TVA** is added to the price of most goods and services in France. You can obtain a refund on purchases of 2000 FF or more at one store (purchases may be combined at department stores). The refund is from 10% to 22%, depending on the items purchased. When you leave France, at Customs (*Douane*), present the items you bought, the bills and the VAT refund forms filled out at the store. Customs will keep both pink sheets of paper, mailing one in the envelope given to you at the store, and will give you the validated green page which you should keep in case of a problem. This documentation **must** be processed at the airport customs counters (or by the train's customs officer if leaving France by rail, or at border customs if driving) **before** luggage is checked because you must show the France-purchased merchandise. Refunds are mailed a few weeks later or credited to your charge card.

☞ **HINT: A new company can help through the refund maze. This service is now available in over 70,000 European stores. For a fee of 15% to 20% of the VAT refund, they will assist you with the paperwork. Send a stamped, self-addressed envelope to Europe Tax-Free Shopping (ETS), 111 W. Monroe St., Suite 2100E, Chicago, IL 60603, tel: 312-346-9126, for a list of participating stores and an explanation of services.**

Water: Most visitors use bottled water for drinking purposes.

Rules of the Road

* Plan the route by checking *Walking Easy in the French Alps* and local hiking maps before you begin the walk.

* Ask about local weather conditions and adjust the day's activities accordingly.

* Always tell someone about your planned route, either a friend or someone at the hotel.

* Take your time, especially at higher altitudes—alpine walking is not a race. Walking at a slow, steady pace provides time for enjoyment of the trail and the scenery.

* Never leave the marked trail.

* Turning back is not a disgrace—if you feel the trail is too difficult, return on the same path or check public transportation in the area.

* In case of an accident, stay calm and send for help. If this is not possible, use the standard alpine distress signal with your whistle or flashlight: six signals, spaced evenly within one minute, pause for one minute, then repeat.

* Many wildflowers are protected by law. Appreciate their beauty, but do not pick them. Leave them for others to enjoy.

* Don't litter. Take out what you bring in. Carry plastic bags in your backpack for this purpose.

* Close any gate you've opened. You don't want to be responsible for the livestock straying.

* Avoid superfluous noise, such as radio-playing, so you don't disturb the animals in their native habitat.

* Avoid forest fires—don't set campfires.

The purpose of any walking trip is to have fun.

So...take a hike...you can do it!

Explanation of Symbols

All walks can be accomplished by a recreational walker of any age, in good health. The following *Walking Easy* symbols are displayed at the beginning of each walk:

Gentle lower-level walks with few ascents and descents, usually through valleys, around lakes, and along rivers on wide paths.

Comfortable ascents and descents over mixed terrain, trails can be narrower.

More challenging ascents and descents, narrow paths with some rocky areas on parts of the trail.

Trail Maps are visual indications of the walking route and are **NOT** drawn to scale.

CHAMONIX

Of the dozens of internationally famous, year-round sports resorts in Europe, none evokes the sheer excitement and instant recognition of the Haute-Savoie's Chamonix. Surrounded by many of Europe's highest peaks, Chamonix at 3402 ft. (1037 m.) is nestled under Mont Blanc's 15,772 ft. (4807 m.) and the Aguilles Rouges at 9728 ft. (2965 m.)—all intertwined with two dozen dramatic glaciers in Pays du Mont Blanc or Mont Blanc Country.

The Tunnel du Mont Blanc wends its way beneath the Mont Blanc massif across the border to Courmayeur, Italy, and serves as an express route to the Aosta Valley, Milan and other popular Italian destinations. Chamonix is easily accessible by car and train, less than two hours driving time from Geneva, Switzerland, with day trips easily arranged to Lausanne and Montreux in Switzerland, Gran Paradiso National Park and Aosta in Italy, and beautiful Lake Annecy.

Chamonix's population of 10,000 includes the neighboring hamlets of Argentière, Montroc, le Tour, le Lavancher, les Praz, les Tines and les Bossons. This superb alpine area supports almost every summer sports activity imaginable: hiking, golf, summer bobsledding and skiing, fishing, swimming, paragliding, rafting, cycling, rock climbing and tennis. The Chamonix Valley is lined with lifts, originally built to service winter skiers. Today these lifts also bring thousands of summer hikers to trails traversing the north and south *balcons* (balconies) on the heights along the Arve River, running swiftly through the valley.

There are dozens of hikes in the Chamonix area, many to be accomplished by *Easy Walkers*. Several hikes are combined with excursions to high, panoramic lookouts, while others use mountain railroads or begin with breathtaking cable car rides over glaciers and high, craggy rock formations. Many of the itineraries take *Easy Walkers* to remote mountain restaurants (*refuges*) for refreshment and relaxation before the walk back to Chamonix.

A "must do" *Walking Easy* hike is the excursion to the Swiss border, using gondola and chairlift from le Tour to Col de Balme—encompassing magnificent views of the Chamonix Valley and Mont Blanc from the east. Large cable cars carrying up to 100 sightseers, climbers and hikers operate during the summer to the Aiguille du Midi at 12,599 ft. (3840 m.), Chamonix's most popular destination, with the option of a breathtaking gondola ride to Helbronner, and even further on to Courmayeur, Italy, on the opposite side of the Mont Blanc massif. Other excursions and walks utilize the Tramway du Mont Blanc, a little yellow and blue mountain train climbing at a 25-degree angle of ascent, which can be boarded at several different stations.

The Chamonix valley has something for everyone: walking, sightseeing excursions, shopping, authentic country cooking and the hospitality of the French Haute-Savoie. Chamonix is the "grandaddy" of walking in the French Alps and is a **must** base village on any *Walking Easy* itinerary in the French Alps.

Transportation to Chamonix

By Plane: The closest international airport to Chamonix is 51 miles (85 km) east at Geneva, Switzerland, with regular train and bus connections through St. Gervais into Chamonix and a wide selection of car rental agencies at the airport. If you find it necessary to fly in and out of Milan,

Italy, a six-hour train ride will bring you into Chamonix, with changes of train in Brig and Martigny in Switzerland and Vallorcine, France. Flying into Paris is, of course, also a fine option.

By Car: From Geneva airport to Chamonix, take super-highway A40 southeast, following signs to Chamonix.

From Charles de Gaulle Airport to Chamonix: from the car rental area in the airport, follow the exit (*sentier*) signs towards Paris. Once out of the airport, immediately follow signs towards Marne la Valleé, then to Lyon on A104, all the way to A6, still in the direction of Lyon.

While it is possible to drive the 381 miles (614 km) to Chamonix in one day, we do not recommend driving for more than three hours after a tiring international flight. Once on A6, you will pass signs to Fountainbleau, Auxerre and Vézelay, followed by the exit to Avallon, and a nice, three-star hotel and restaurant a few minutes from the Avallon exit. With a gasoline/lunch/rest stop, it should take about three hours from the airport to Avallon. After paying the express-way toll, take the first right turn in the direction of Avallon, and within a few minutes you will see a sign for the hotel. (See the "Accommodations" chapter for more details on lodging here.)

After a good night's rest, continue driving on A6 south towards Lyon, leaving the highway at Macon on A40 in the direction of Bourg-en-Bresse. Continue on A40, a major highway, past Geneva to Chamonix, following the signs to Chamonix/Mont Blanc.

By Train: TGV (high-speed trains) are regularly scheduled to and from Paris, with a change of train in Annecy, to the St-Gervais station, 12 miles (20 km) from Chamonix. There are several daily trains to and from Lyon, Marseilles and Nice to Chamonix, and connections with main lines of the Swiss

Railway system through Martigny. Chamonix is on the Le Fayet-Chamonix-Vallorcine line from Geneva and Annecy. When traveling to Chamonix from Switzerland, there is always a change of train in Martigny, Switzerland.

Sample Train Schedules

Dep. Paris	7:09 am (TGV)
Arr. St-Gervais	12:38 pm
Dep. St-Gervais	1:04 pm
Arr. Chamonix	1:42 pm
Dep. Milan	12:24 pm
Arr. Brig	2:40 pm
Dep. Brig	3:07 pm
Arr. Martigny	4:07 pm
Dep. Martigny	4:38 pm
Arr. Vallorcine	5:38 pm
Dep. Vallorcine	6:08 pm
Arr. Chamonix	6:39 pm
Dep. Geneva	11:10 am
Arr. St-Gervais	12:38 pm
Dep. St-Gervais	1:04 pm
Arr. Chamonix	1:44 pm
Dep. Geneva	11:48 am
Arr. Martigny	1:24 pm
Dep. Martigny	1:30 pm
Arr. Chamonix	3:08 pm

Local Public Transportation: The convenient yellow-and-blue municipal bus line operates regular shuttle service throughout the Chamonix valley. The Chamonix bus leaves from the bus station next to the Chamonix Tourist Office for stops in le Tour, les Houches, Argentière, Col des Montets, etc. Pick up a bus schedule and bus stop map at the booth by the main station—fare is 7 FF for each trip section.

Activities in Chamonix

This section lists activities available in Chamonix on days when additions or alternatives to walking are desired. The busy and helpful Chamonix/Mont Blanc Tourist Bureau (Office du Tourisme) on Place du Triangle de l'Amitié, across from the church, is open daily from 8:30 am to 7:30 pm, tel: 50-53-00-24.

From June 15th to September 15th, the "Pass'sports + The Mountain" card offers 10% discounts on lifts and sports activities. The card contains 22 tickets (each ticket worth 20 FF), and is sold for 400 FF at the Sports Club or Sports Center.

Aguilles Rouges Nature Reserve - The reserve is located at Col des Montets and contains many acres of flora and fauna, including a nature trail with volunteer guides. There are lectures and guided visits every Thursday, but call 50-54-02-24 for the availability of English tours.

Alpine Animal Park - This zoo is located at Merlet towards les Houches. Visit alpine animals in natural, open surroundings. (See Walk #3 for more details.)

Alpine Museum - The museum is located at la Résidence in the walking area of Chamonix. It is open every day from 2:00 pm to 7:00 pm and contains collections on the history of the Chamonix Valley—skiing, mountaineering, minerology, cartography, also engravings, lithographs and old posters.

Casino - The casino is situated on Place de Saussure in the town center, with French and English roulette, blackjack and punto banco. It's open from 8:00 pm to 4:00 am weekdays, and opens at 5:00 pm on weekends.

Cycling and Mountain Biking - See Club des Sports at the Tourist Office for special routes and maps. Bikes are available for rent at various sports stores.

Fishing - Fishing is permitted in nearby streams and lakes, and fishing licenses can be obtained from Les Sport Verts, tel: 50-53-42-13.

Golf - The golf course is at les Praz, less than two miles (3 km) from town center. It is an 18-hole, par 72 course, with clubs, carts and bags for rent. Telephone 50-53-06-28 for tee times and information.

Helicopter Rides - Call S.A.F. Chamonix Helicopters at 50-54-07-86, or Chamonix Mont-Blanc Helicoptères at 50-54-13-82.

Horseback Riding - Riding is available at Club Hippique "La Guérinière" in les Pélerins d'en Haut, tel: 50-53-06-72.

Ice Skating - An indoor rink with rental skates available is located at the Sports Center, open 3:00 pm to 8:00 pm every day and until 11:00 pm on Wednesdays.

Mont-Blanc Observatory - 67, Lacets du Belvédère. The observatory is open to the public from July 19 to September 4. Call 50-53-45-16 for information about programs.

Paragliding - Call Club des Sport at 50-53-11-57.

Swimming - Olympic indoor and outdoor pools are located at the Sports Center, open 10:00 am to 8:00 pm weekdays and until 10:00 pm Fridays.

Tennis - 18 tennis courts are available, six of them indoors. Call 50-53-28-40 for reservations and information.

Excursions in and around Chamonix

This section introduces day excursions that *Easy Walkers* will enjoy when an alternative to walking is desired. Be sure to check current timetables for best connections if public transportation is used.

1. Lifts in and around Chamonix

A) Mer de Glace (Sea of Ice) - Take a mountain cog railway from Chamonix's Gare du Montenvers to Europe's second-largest glacier at 6313 ft. (1924 m.). Visit the glacier by walking down the steep path or by taking the small cable car. *Easy Walkers* will enjoy the Ice Grotto, at a depth of 200 ft. (80 m.) into the glacier. Four months of work each spring create new scuptures in an eerie, sub-glacial atmosphere. (See Walk #1 for more details.)

Directions: Take the Montenvers cog railway, located to the left when facing the Chamonix railroad station (Gare SNCF). It runs every half-hour.

B) Aiguille du Midi - This is an exciting two-stage cable car—the first stage rises to 7602 ft. (2317 m.), with the second stage a nearly vertical ascent to the summit of the Aiguille at 12,600 ft. (3840 m.). Cross the footbridge between Piton Nord and Piton Central when you arrive and walk to the Mont Blanc Terrace for stunning, panoramic views. Walk through the ice tunnel of the Galerie de la Vallée Blanche, on your left after the footbridge, to catch sight of fully equipped mountain climbers beginning or ending their trips into the Vallée Blanche.

 HINT: Walk slowly—you are at 12,600 ft. (3840 m.), and the high altitude can cause dizziness. If this occurs, sit down and rest for ten to fifteen minutes to adjust.

If the weather is clear, you can continue your trip into the high mountains by taking the gondola from Aiguille du Midi to Helbronner, an exciting three-mile (5-km) ride over the ice of the Géant glacier. During this trip the gondola slows down five times to allow for picture taking! Remember, do not take this part of the trip unless the weather is clear. Note, too, that the top of the Aiguille is cold. Put those insulated jackets into your backpack! (See Walk #4 for more details.)

Directions: Walk west through town on the main street Rue Joseph Vallot, past the Post Office on Rue du Dr. Paccard, following the sign to Aiguille du Midi.

C) Le Tour - A 14-minute ride to the top station (Col de Balme) at 7153 ft. (2180 m.) is interrupted only by a quick change at the mid-station from a six-person gondola to a four-place, open chairlift. (See Walk #7 for more details.)

Directions: Take the Chamonix bus to the last stop at le Tour and buy a round-trip ticket to the top station.

D) Les Bossons - This chairlift rises to 4626 ft. (1410 m.) and takes you along the side of the magnificent Bossons glacier, a focal point of the scenery around Chamonix. (See Walk #6 for more details.)

Directions: At the main Chamonix bus stop across from the Tourist Office, take the bus towards les Houches, asking to be let off at les Bossons chairlift.

E) La Flégère - Starting from 6158 ft. (1877 m.), this cable car rises to l'Index at 8285 ft. (2525 m.) and descends to les Praz at 3478 ft. (1060 m.), providing superb views of Mer de Glace and the Chamonix valley. (See Walk #2 for more details.)

Directions: Take the Chamonix bus in the direction of le Tour and exit at la Flégère.

F) Le Brévant - This two-stage gondola and cable car ascends first to Planpraz at 6562 ft. (2000 m.), then the second stage rises to le Brévant at 8285 ft. (2525 m.). The views from the top to les Bossons glacier and the Mont Blanc massif are exhilarating. (See Walk #2 for more details.)

Directions: Walk into town, past the Tourist Office and the church, straight up the hill, following signs to le Brévant.

G) Tramway du Mont Blanc - The Tramway du Mont Blanc has a long history of development, with work finished to the terminus at Nid d'Aigle in 1913. The engineers' original intention was to bring this tramway to the summit of Mont Blanc, but their goal was interrupted by World War I and the railroad was never finished. Today this is an exciting mountain train ride from Col de Voza up to Nid d'Aigle at 7783 ft. (2372 m.) with views over the Glacier de Bionnassy. (See Walk #6 for more details.)

Directions: At the central Chamonix bus station, take the bus to les Houches. Exit at the last stop in les Houches and take the gondola up to le Prarion. From here, walk uphill past the Prarion Hotel and, following the signed directions, to Col de Voza. Turn left at the wide trail for the 25-minute walk down to Col de Voza and the tramway du Mont Blanc station. Or, check with the Tourist Office for other stops on the tram.

2. Evian-les-Bains - Situated on the shores of Lake Geneva (Lac Léman), Evian is 65 miles (104 km) north of Chamonix. World-famous "Evian" water was discovered here in the 19th century and turned a small, heavily fortified town into a Belle Epoque health spa with magnificent hotels and sculptured gardens. From Evian, many boat trips are available, and while a cruise of the entire lake takes ten hours, it is only a 35-minute boat ride to Lausanne/Ouchy or Montreux and Chillon Castle, on the Swiss side of the lake.

(See Excursions #5 and #6 for more details on these Swiss destinations.)

Directions: By car - Take N205 west out of Chamonix into Cluses, turning right on D902 into Thonons. Drive east on N5 into Evian. For a return circle route, drive east out of Evian on N5, crossing the Swiss border at St. Gingolph, then driving south to Monthey. Go east towards Bex and then south to Martigny where you will pick up N506 through the Col de la Forclaz and over the French border into Chamonix. A bus excursion to Lake Geneva, Evian, Thonon, le Chablais and Morzine is available with the Chamonix Bus Excursions company located across from the Tourist Office. The bus leaves at 8:00 am and arrives back in Chamonix at 7:00 pm.

☞ **HINT: Remember your passport if you plan on leaving France for this or any other excursion or walk!**

3. Megève - Located about 22 miles (35 km) southwest of Chamonix, Megève is another major French ski resort and *Walking Easy* base village, overflowing with trendy boutiques and outdoor cafés, its downtown area bisected by an alpine stream. If you aren't going to stay in Megève, plan to visit on a Friday when the mountain farmers sell local produce at an outdoor market next to the sports center. (See the "Megève" chapter for more details.)

Directions: By car - Drive E25-N205 west to St. Gervais, following signs to Albertville and Mégève. Take N212 into Megève.

4. Annecy - Annecy has been called "The Venice of the Alps" because of canals cut through the old section of town. This "Jewel of the Savoy Alps" is now a major urban center on Lac d'Annecy, but its old town is charming and well-preserved, spanning the Thiou River as it leaves the lake. From one of its many bridges, note the **Palais de l'Ile**, a former prison, rising from the stream like the prow of a ship. Walk on **Rue Ste-Claire**, a lovely old street with arcades and 17th-century gabled buildings. Visit **Château Annecy**, former residence of the Counts of Geneva and the Dukes of Savoie-Nemours, open every day from 10:00 am to noon and 2:00 pm to 6:00 pm, with admission charge. On the last Saturday of each month Annecy hosts a flea and antiques market in the old city.

The lake itself can be seen best from Avenue d'Albigny—enjoy this lovely body of water set in a glacial valley, surrounded by the Bauges massif to the south and gentle, rolling hills northwest towards Geneva. Walk around the popular lakefront and visit the **casino** if you are so inclined. If time permits, steamers leave Annecy for tours around the lake.

One noteworthy side excursion from Annecy is a visit to **Les Gorges du Fier**, six miles (10 km) away, 12 minutes by train from the Lovagny railroad station on the Aix-les-Bains line. Visitors make their way into the depths of this gorge on platforms winding through rocks and torrents, and find an immense field of boulders upon exiting the chasm. It is open daily from 9:00 am to 6:00 pm, and admission is charged for the one-hour walking tour.

Directions: By car - Take E25-N205 west out of Chamonix to St. Gervais, picking up N212 through Megève to Aciéries where you take N508 towards Ugine. Drive through Faverges and continue around the left side of the lake to Annecy. You can return to Chamonix on a circle route by way of N203 out of Annecy through St. Martin-Bellevue, veering east to superhighway A40 outside of Passeirier, following signs to Chamonix. By bus - A bus leaves Chamonix at 7:00 am, arriving in Annecy at 9:30 am. To return, take the 3:30 pm bus, arriving in Chamonix at 6:10 pm. Or, take a Chamonix Bus Excursion, leaving at 8:00 am and arriving back in Chamonix at 6:30 pm.

5. Montreux, Switzerland - Sometimes called "The Vaud Riviera," this, the most popular resort on Lake Geneva (Lac Léman), is noted for its mild weather, producing a Mediterranean feeling in summer. Enjoy the path that runs for miles along the lake shore, planted with all types of semi-tropical plants and flowers—a wonderful contrast to the snowy scenery and wintery pine forests around Chamonix.

The **Castle of Chillon**, made famous by the poet Byron, is only one and one-half miles (2.5 km) from Montreux. Check at the Montreux train station for a bus schedule to the castle. From the Montreux railroad station, *Easy Walkers* can also take an excursion by mountain railroad to **Rochers de Naye** at 7002 ft. (2134 m.) for a spectacular view of the lake, ringed by the French and Swiss Alps. There are also numerous pleasant walking paths winding through the countryside. Allow one hour each way for the train trip to Rochers de Naye.

Directions: By car - Follow N506 northeast from Chamonix, over the Swiss border, through Col de la Forclaz, to Martigny. Take highway N9 into Montreux, following signs to Lausanne. A Chamonix Excursion Bus leaves Chamonix at 1:00 pm, goes to Montreux and Chillon, and returns to Chamonix at 6:30 pm.

6. Lausanne, Switzerland - Lausanne's **cathedral** is reputedly the most beautiful Gothic building in Switzerland—its picturesque towers and sculptured doors date from 1175 to 1275. The cathedral boasts one of the last "watches" in the world, whose duty it is to cry the hours from 10:00 pm to 2:00 am. Lausanne is home to the first museum in French-speaking Switzerland devoted solely to modern art, the **FAE Museum of Contemporary Art**, on the shore of Lake Geneva in Pully, about ten minutes from the city center. Ouchy, a bustling port on Lake Geneva, is now the lakefront for Lausanne, originally built up and away from the lake. Ouchy's shady piers provide delightful views over the port, the lake and the mountains.

Directions: By car - Take N506 northeast out of Chamonix, over the Swiss boarder and through Col de la Forclaz to Martigny. Pick up highway N9, past Montreux and Vevey, around Lake Geneva into Lausanne.

7. Courmayeur, Italy - This well-known summer and winter resort at the foot of the Mont Blanc massif sits at an altitude of 4029 ft. (1228 m.). You can take the cable car from Courmayeur to Plan Chécrouit, rise to Altiporto, then to Cresta di Youla, where another cable car climbs to Cresta d'Arp at 9065 ft. (2763 m.). Enjoy a splendid panorama of alpine peaks, including Mont Blanc to the north and the Matterhorn and Monte Rosa to the northeast. Allow at least two hours round-trip for traveling time.

About two miles (3 km) north of Courmayeur is **la Palud**, where you can ride the cable car up to Mont Blanc, crossing into France. The viewing platform at Helbronner is over 11,000 ft. (3353 m.) and is also the border with France. The next stage brings you over immense glacial snow fields and to a viewing station above Chamonix. If you change cable cars you can ride directly down to Chamonix! (See Walk #4 for more details.)

Directions: By car - Drive through the Tunnel du Mt. Blanc, continuing straight ahead on S26 into Courmayeur. By bus - The 9:15 or 10:05 am bus from Chamonix arrives in Courmayeur at 9:55 or 10:45 am. To return, there are 3:30 and 5:10 pm departing buses, arriving in Chamonix at 4:10 or 5:50 pm.

8. Gran Paradiso National Park, Italy - Created in 1922 and covering 1390 square miles (60,000 hectares), this park originated as the Italian royal family's hunting preserve and is now one of Europe's treasured wilderness areas. Its wildlife and flowers are protected by law so that many threatened species are thriving in the park. The park's alpine garden is at Valmontey, containing over 2000 species of flowers, as well as moors, marshland, lakes and streams. The Gran Paradiso extends to the west and in France becomes the Parc National de la Vanoise. If you wish to walk in the Gran Paradiso, contact experienced walking guides Claire and Eric Thioliere at the Hotel Sapinière. They will take you into Gran Paradiso with a return to Chamonix.

Directions: By car - Drive through the Mont Blanc Tunnel, continuing straight ahead on S26, through Courmayeur and into the Aosta Valley towards Aosta. Make a right turn at Aymavilles, about four miles (6 km) west of Aosta, climbing into the Val di Cogne. The village of Cogne at 5033 ft. (1534 m.) is 12 miles (20 km) up into the valley, a good place to stop and enjoy the beauty and solitude of the park. The Chamonix Excursion Bus can take you to Parc National du Gran Paradis and Vallee de Cogne et ses Dentellieres. It leaves at 9:00 am and arrives back in Chamonix at 6:30 pm.

9. Aosta, Italy - This small city is the capital of the Aosta Valley, and its Roman ruins make it a popular tourist destination. The most important of these ancient relics are the **Pretoria Gateway (Porta Pretoria)**, three arches built of huge blocks of stone in 1 BC; the **Arch of Augustus (Arco di Augusto)**, built in 25 BC when Rome defeated the Celtic Salassi tribe; and the **Roman Bridge.** From the Pretoria Gateway you can reach the remains of the **Roman theater (teatro Romano)** and a recently discovered **Roman road**.

Collegiate Church of St. Orso (Collegiata di Sant'Orso) boasts an 11th-century crypt and a 12th-century Roman bell tower. A rich treasure of sacred art and paintings is kept in the sacristy. Nearby is a small Romanesque **cloister**, dating back to the 12th century. The **cathedral (duomo)** is ornamented with 16th-century sculptures on its 19th-century facade, however, the rest of the church dates from the 12th to the 15th centuries. Opposite the cathedral stands the ruins of a **Roman forum.**

Directions: By car - Take the Mont Blanc Tunnel and drive though Courmayeur on S26, continuing east into Aosta. By bus - The Chamonix Excursion Bus departs for Aosta at 1:00 pm and is back in Chamonix at 7:00 pm. There is also a Chamonix public bus at 10:05 am that arrives in Aosta at 11:40 am. To return, you can take the 5:45 bus from Aosta, arriving in Chamonix at 6:30 pm.

10. Geneva, Switzerland - Geneva's Tourist Office is near the downtown railroad station on place Cornavin and can provide *Easy Walkers* with information about the city, along with an indispensible city map. Geneva is divided by Lake Geneva and the Rhône River into two sections, the right and the left bank. The old town of Geneva is on the left bank—with Gothic, Renaissance and 18th-century buildings, narrow alleyways and cascading fountains. Geneva's top attractions are the famous water fountain that has become the city's symbol, the **Jet d'Eau**; the **flower clock** in the Jardin Anglais; the **old town**; and its **museums**.

The **Museum of Art and History (Musée D'Art et D'Histoire)**, 2, rue Charles-Galland, displays prehistoric relics, Greek vases, medieval stained glass, Swiss watches and clocks, paintings, etc. It is open Tuesday to Sunday from 10:00 am to 5:00 pm, admission free. Take bus 3 or 33.

Musée International de la Croix-Rouge et du Croissant-Rouge, on 17, av. de la Paix, presents the history of the Red Cross. It is open every day but Tuesday from 10:00 am to 5:00 pm, with admission charge. Take bus 8 or F.

Palais des Nations in the Parc de l'Ariana, is the second largest complex of buildings in Europe after Versailles. It is United Nations headquarters in Europe and also contains a **Philatelic Museum** and the **League of Nations Mu-**

seum. From June to October it is open daily from 9:00 am to 5:15 pm. Take bus 8 or F.

The **Watch Museum (Musée de l'Horlogerie)** is at 15, route de Malagnou and displays everything relating to clocks and watches—from sun-dials to modern exhibitions. It is open Wednesday to Monday from 10:00 am to 5:00 pm, admission free. Take bus 6.

In the **old town** the dominating feature is **Cathédrale de Saint-Pierre**, built in the 12th and 13th centuries and renovated in the 15th century and again over the years. You can climb 45 stairs to the top of the north tower for a great view of the city, the lake, and the distant Alps. The tower is open daily from 11:30 am to 5:30 pm, with admission charge. The cathedral and the chapel are open daily from 9:00 am to 7:00 pm.

Geneva has a wonderful public transportation system beginning at place Cornavin, in front of the main railroad station. No tickets are sold on buses or trams—you must buy them at the coin-operated vending machines at each stop. The three types of tickets are:

1) Free transportation for one hour, with as many changes as you want, on any type of vehicle:1.50 SF.

2) Trip limited to three stops (no change of vehicle): .90 SF.

3) Rides for one hour for seniors (women over 62 and men over 65): .80 SF.

4) One-day tickets good on any line: 6 SF.

All tickets must be validated at the vending machine before entering the bus or tram.

Directions: By car - Take N205 west out of Chamonix, picking up highway A40 to the outskirts of Geneva. Follow signs to the city center. By bus - An 8:00 bus from Chamonix arrives in Geneva at 10:05 am. To return, there is a 5:20 bus arrving in Chamonix at 7:30 pm. Or, you can take the

9:00 am Chamonix Excursion Bus, arriving back in Chamonix at 6:30 pm.

11. Great St. Bernard Pass/Hospice, Switzerland - The Hospice stands at 8100 ft. (2469 m.), the highest point on the Great Saint Bernard Pass and Road, now bypassed by a new tunnel. On the edge of a lake frozen 265 days a year, the Hospice is the home of the grand, gentle dogs noted for carrying brandy to travelers stranded in the mountain snows. The **chapel**, with its pulpits and stalls dating from the 17th century, and the **museum's** pictures and memorabilia, should be visited. The famous **Grand Saint Bernard dogs** who accompanied the monks on their rescue missions are in the kennels behind the hotel. Today, since helicopters have taken their place, the dogs sleep most of the day!

There is an enjoyable walking trail overlooking the small lake and ending at the customs station in Italy. As you leave the museum, pick up the path above the road on the right side. After a few minutes you'll see a sign indicating Italy! Continue maneuvering on the narrow, rocky, descending trail, allowing entrance into Italy and bypassing the customs station. Within a few minutes you'll be at the souvenir stands on the Italian side of the border. To return to the Hospice, walk back up the road, through the customs stations.

Directions: By car - Take the Mt. Blanc Tunnel outside of Chamonix and pick up S26 through Courmayeur, west to Aosta. Drive north on S27 but do **not** drive through the St. Bernard Tunnel—take the old, winding road to the Hospice, right over the Swiss border. For a circle route to return, continue north on 21 into Martigny and take N506 west into Chamonix. The Chamonix Excursion Bus leaves Chamonix at 8:00 am for Col de la Forclaz, Bourg Saint-Pierre, Grand Saint-Bernard and Aosta, and is back in Chamonix at 6:30.

12. Sion, Switzerland - As you approach Sion, two rocky hills dominate the landscape. A ruined fortress (**Tourbillon**) is on one hill. On the other hill (**Valère**), stands a church containing the oldest playable organ in the world, built in 1390. Walk on Sion's narrow, old streets and visit the **Sorcerer's Tower** and the 17th-century **town hall** with its magnificent carved doors and astronomical clock. Many example of Celtic, Roman and medieval art and artifacts can be found in the **Cathedral Notre Dame du Glarier**. The views from the top of the two hills with their Disney-like ruins are excellent, but **Valère**, with its castle, basilica, organ and museum, should not be missed.

Directions: By car - Take N506 northeast out of Chamonix, crossing the Swiss border into Martigny. Pick up 9 towards Brig and drive east into Sion.

13. Sierre, Switzerland - This town is situated in the heart of the wine district of the Valais region, and the local Tourist Office can supply maps for walks through the surrounding vineyards. Sierre is one of the sunniest and driest cities in Switzerland, with more than 200 days of sunshine and only 24 inches of rain per year. Walk on the **Rue du Bourg** and explore the old quarter. Notice a 15th-century **tower castle**, a 12th-century **monastery**, a 13th-century **tower house**, and the Gothic **Church of Notre Dame des Marais**. An interesting note: in this part of Switzerland, the language changes from French to German.

Directions: By car - Follow N506 northeast out of Chamonix, over the Swiss border into Martigny. Take 9 towards Brig, past Sion into Sierre.

14. Zermatt, Switzerland - A tourist and hiking mecca, Zermatt's surrounding mountains and glaciers encompass superb scenery, including the mighty and famous Matterhorn. An abundance of railroads and cable cars reaching the tops of Zermatt's high, snow-capped mountains makes this town a wonderful place for a long day trip from Chamonix. You can pass the time in a trendy mix of souvenir shops and cosmopolitan boutiques, restaurants and small cafés, or choose any of the following exciting sightseeing options:

A) Gornergrat Cog Railway - The entrance is across the street from the Zermatt Railroad Station. A 45-minute trip on the highest rack railway in Europe brings *Easy Walkers* to Gornergrat at 10,272 ft. (3131 m.), with a fabulous view of the Matterhorn and the spectacular sight of Monte Rosa and its glaciers, at 15,203 ft. (4634 m.), the highest mountain in Switzerland. At the Gornergrat stop, with its Kulm Hotel, a restaurant and large, outdoor terrace are frequently filled with skiers, hikers, climbers and sun-worshippers. From here *Easy Walkers* can continue up to the Stockhorn peak at 11,588 ft. (3532 m.) by a 22-minute cable car ride, for an awe-inspiring, glacial panorama.

B) Klein Matterhorn Cable Car - Turn right on leaving the Zermatt railroad station, walk up the tourist-filled main street through town to the church, turn left, and you will arrive at the famous Zermatt cemetery. This well-tended cemetery serves as a testimonial to those climbers who lost their lives trying to scale the heights of the region's mountains. The tombstones spell out the history and courage of men of all ages and countries who tried to conquer the Matterhorn and failed. Passing the cemetery, cross the river and turn right, where a short walk brings you to the lift station.

Easy Walkers can spend an hour and take four different and connecting cable cars to reach the top of the Klein Matterhorn, at 12,684 ft. (3866 m.), the highest-altitude cable car station in Europe. The view of the Alps from France to Austria is breathtaking. Descending, the foot of the famed Matterhorn is your destination—its peak is reflected in the still waters of the Schwarzsee, a tiny mountain lake at an elevation of 8500 ft. (2591 m.).

C) Sunnegga Underground Railway - After arriving in Zermatt, walk straight ahead and follow signs to the Sunnegga Express Station. Sunnegga sits at 7500 ft. (2286 m.) on a high, alpine plateau, with a southwest view of the Matterhorn and panoramic vistas of mountains, glaciers, valleys and lakes. The underground railway takes 20 minutes to reach the Sunnegga station. From Sunnegga, a cable car continues up to Blauherd at 8620 ft. (2627 m.), where a second cable car takes riders to the rocky summit of the 10,180 foot (3103 m.) Unter Rothorn with exceptional views of the Findel Glacier, the Matterhorn and Zermatt.

Directions: By car (leave **very** early in the morning!) - Follow N506 northeast out of Chamonix, crossing the Swiss border to Martigny. Take 9 towards Brig, past Sion and Sierre, into Visp. You can catch a train into Zermatt at Visp or drive further on 215 south to Täsch, parking your car in the giant parking area and taking the short train ride to traffic-free Zermatt. A bus and train excursion to Zermatt is available by Chamonix Bus Excursions, leaving Chamonix at 7:30 am and arriving back in Chamonix at 7:30 pm. Check at the excursion booth across from the Tourist Office.

Chamonix Walks

Recommended Maps:
1) Carte des Sentiers de Montagne en Été - Mont Blanc/Chamonix
2) IGN Chamonix, 3630 OT

Walk #1: Plan de l'Aiguille to Mer de Glace (Excursion to Mer de Glace and Ice Grotto)

Walking Easy Time
3 to 5 hours

Today's hike is one of the more sensational walks in the Chamonix area. The trail goes along the Gran Balcon Nord overlooking Chamonix, the valley, its neighboring villages and the mountains on the opposite side of the valley, where additional walks will be taken on other days. This is a full day's excursion and utilizes the first section of the Aiguille du Midi cable lift, exiting at its mid-station. (For those who are not planning to do Walk #4, this might be a good opportunity to take the second section of the cable car to Aiguille du Midi, returning to

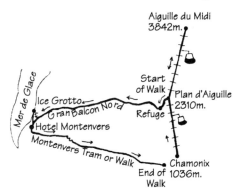

mid-station Plan de l'Aiguille for the beginning of today's walk.) At Plan de l'Aiguille at 7579 ft. (2310 m.), overlooking the dramatic Bossons glacier, you will walk along the Gran Balcon Nord to Mer de Glace, one of Europe's largest glaciers, where it is possible to visit the glacier by descending in a small lift. The return to Chamonix is by the quaint Montenvers mountain railroad or by a pleasant walking descent through the forest to the valley floor.

Directions: Walk through town to the Aiguille du Midi cable car, easily found on the town map. Purchase a ticket to the mid-station, Plan de l'Aiguille—unless you wish to visit the Aiguille du Midi today. Due to the popularity of this lift an early start is suggested. On busy days, your ticket will have the time and number of the cable car you've been assigned to. Take the lift to mid-station Plan de l'Aiguille and exit the car for the start of today's walk.

Start: Walk through the exit and turn left, following the steep trail down the mountain on a well-beaten path, for about ten minutes, to the little restaurant/*refuge* Plan de l'Aiguille. This walk down to the restaurant should be taken slowly. It is the steepest part of today's hike but only takes a short time.

Follow the signs at the side of the restaurant to Mer de Glace. This often rocky path will take you across the mountain to another glacier on a well-trafficked, open trail, with views of the towering, jagged formations of the Aiguille on the right and Chamonix and the valley down on your left. There are some side trails descending steeply down to Chamonix—do **not** take them.

The walk rambles in and around 6562 ft. (2000 m.) and descends to 6156 ft. (1908 m.) at the Hotel Montenvers. Bear to the right at the hotel and within minutes you will arrive at the awesome sight of one of Europe's largest glaciers, the Mer de Glace, literally, the Sea of Ice. The Mer de Glace is almost nine miles (14 km) long and is the second largest glacier in the Alps. Like all glaciers, it moves (!), this one at about 295 ft. (90 m.) per year. It is possible to take a small cable car down for a visit to the glacier and the ice grotto. Ice artists work months in the spring preparing ice sculptures that look magical in the eerie blue light of the subglacial atmosphere.

To return to Chamonix, you might wish to board the Montenvers train for the 20-minute return ride down. The last stop of the Montenvers train is adjacent to the Chamonix railroad station. A walk back to your hotel ends an unusual day hiking from one imposing glacier to another—Bossons glacier to Mer de Glace. A walk down to Chamonix on the wide mule-path trail through the forest is also a nice way to end this exciting day. Judge your time and scheduling carefully, and if you decide on this two-hour hiking option, follow signs at Mer de Glace to Chamonix.

Walk #2: Excursion to Brévant, Walk Planpraz to La Flégère and Les Praz to Chamonix

Walking Easy Time
3½ hours

Today's walk/excursion will take most of the day, so you should be on the road by 9:30 am. You will walk from Chamonix center to the Brévant cable car where the second section of the lift takes you to the Brévant peak. After viewing the magnificent panorama of the Mont Blanc massif, you will return by the same cable car to the Planpraz mid-station where the walk begins. The three-hour hike takes you to the cable car station at la Flégère at 6158 ft. (1877 m.), on a rocky, mountain path with the usual ascents and descents.

The views across the valley over Chamonix are of the famous Mont Blanc massif, with the Glacier des Bossons to the right, as you walk in the direction of Mer de Glace across the valley. You will view 15,772-foot (4807-m.) Mont Blanc and 12,606-foot (3842-m.) Aiguille du Midi, towering over the Bossons glacier as it appears to flow into the Chamonix Valley. As you hike towards la Flégère you will also see the Montenvers Railroad climbing the mountain across the valley towards Mer de Glace. The Mer de Glace, one of the largest glaciers in Europe, will come into view at the terrace of the hotel at la Flégère. You will descend to les Praz at 3478 ft. (1060 m.) by lift and walk to Chamonix along a gentle river path. A picnic lunch might be enjoyable today—although there are restaurants and facilities at each lift station.

Directions: Starting from the Chamonix Tourist Office, walk up past the church, following the signs to the Brévant cable car. This walk is uphill for about ten minutes—take it slowly. Buy a ticket to Brévant with return to Planpraz. Take the gondola to the mid-station and change for the cable car and the short ride to Brévant at 8285 ft. (2525 m.). After viewing the fabulous panorama of the Mont Blanc massif across the valley, catch the next cable car back to mid-station Planpraz at 6559 ft. (1999 m.), where your hike begins.

Start: The first ten minutes of this hike are probably the most challenging. After leaving the cable car station, walk **up** the wide dirt path to signs pointing in the direction of la Flégère. Take this start of your hike slowly and you will soon reach the ski lift station and another sign pointing again towards la Flégère. Walking on a wide, rocky path, stay to the left as you descend. Directional signs continue to confirm the trail towards la Flégère.

After about an hour you will reach Charlanon at 5945 ft. (1812 m.) and a nice meadow for a picnic lunch. The trail continues upwards for a while and then levels off. You will soon see your destination cable station ahead, across the valley from the Mer de Glace, and shortly reach a series of steep, rocky steps with iron railings to aid the ascent.

This ascent lasts for only a few minutes, bringing you to the level trail to the ca-ble station. If it is early, you might wish to take the cable car up to l'Index at 8285 ft. (2525 m.), for a superb view of Mer de Glace and Chamonix valley. If not, purchase a one-way ticket down to les Praz—cable cars leave on the hour and half-hour.

On exiting the cable station at les Praz, turn left to the river, and left again on the signed Chamonix path along the river, the easy walk taking 30 minutes and bringing you past the sports center into the main streets of Chamonix. An alternative to walking the one and one-quarter miles (2 km) back to Chamonix is the Chamonix bus, with a stop outside the parking lot on the street. Buses run about every half-hour—check the posted schedule.

Walk #3: Chamonix to Merlet on Petit Balcon Sud

Walking Easy Time
2 to 4 hours

This medium-level walk brings *Easy Walkers* to unparalleled views of the Bossons glacier, directly across the valley from today's trail. The walk begins at Brévant lift station and proceeds to Merlet along the lower entry to the Petit Balcon Sud. The trail ascends about 328 ft. (100 m.) during the first 45 minutes on a wide, shaded, but rocky path through a cool pine forest, with views of the Bosson Glacier every so often on the left. The trail levels off at about 3937 ft. (1200 m.) in the direction of Merlet, the site of an interesting wild animal park. Walkers have the option of returning on the same path if they feel the last ascent of 1148 ft. (350 m.) to Merlet at 5125 ft. (1562 m.) is too demanding. The path is reasonably well-marked and signed, and *Easy Walkers* will return to Chamonix on the same path. There is an option for the more energetic walker to visit the peak, then continue the hike down to les Houches at 3314 ft. (1010 m.) to catch the bus back to Chamonix.

Start: From the Chamonix Tourist Office, take the ascending auto road past the church, following signs to the Brévant cable car. Walk to the left, past the lift station and tourist stores, and continue on the auto road marked "les Moussoux" in the direction of Merlet. This is the easiest and shortest route to the Petit Balcon Sud— Route des Moussoux. Views of the Bossons glacier will be ahead on the left as you walk on the road through a residential area. After a few minutes you'll see a sign for Petit Balcon Sud, and in about ten minutes the road ends and you enter the forest on a nicely defined trail.

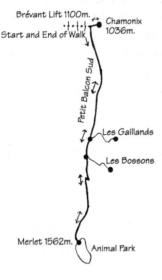

A sign indicates "Merlet - 1 hr. 45 min.," but *Easy Walkers* will take longer. Remember to take the ascents slowly; they will be descents on the way back!

After walking about 35 minutes, do **not** take the descending white-and-red blazed trail on your left. Continue straight ahead, ascending on the main trail where signs continue to point ahead to Merlet. When the path forks again, continue on your left to Merlet, **not** taking the trail to the right up to Plan Lachat. You will pass an entry to a trail on the left marked "les Gaillands" that descends rather rapidly to the valley floor, but *Easy Walkers* will continue on the main trail to Merlet.

When the path takes a sharp right turn, visit the lookout at this point for some remarkable views of the glacier. Continue on the main trail which then buttonhooks back to its original direction towards Merlet. After passing a descending trail to les Bosson on your left, the rate of ascent increases more dramatically until your destination of Merlet is reached. *Easy Walkers*, however, should exercise their option of returning to Chamonix along the same path at any time, descending most of the way on the return.

For those who wish to continue, the ascending path remains well-marked all the way to the animal park, where additional decisions can be made to continue down to les Houches to return to Chamonix by bus, or to return on the same path you walked up on.

Walk #4: Excursion to Aiguille du Midi and Helbronner, Walk to Lac Bleu

 Plan a full day for today's walk and excursion.

This excursion to the Aiguille du Midi is placed in the "Walks" section because the authors wanted to make sure that you did not miss this trip! However, it **must** be taken on the first available clear day of your holiday in Chamonix! There is a small walk to Lac Bleu at the mid-station, but the real purpose of today's outing is a visit to the Aiguille du Midi and the ride over the Glacier du Géant to Helbronner and Italy. Note that there is some planning and preparation necessary for this full day's excursion, as the Aiguille du Midi is the most popular attraction in Chamonix.

☞ HINT: It might be a good idea to book your visit by telephone before you arrive, especially during the month of August. The telephone booking number is

50-53-40-00. For additional information by telephone, call 50-53-30-80.

Start: The trip to the Aiguille du Midi leaves from the lift
station on the outskirts of Chamonix, easily reached by a
short walk from the center
of town. Follow signs and
walk directly to the cashier's
window indicating "reservations," if you made them
earlier. If not, stand in the
adjacent line and purchase a
round-trip ticket from
Chamonix to Helbronner at
11,359 ft. (3462 m.), if the
weather is clear and that is
your goal, or you can short-
en today's outing by just visiting the Aiguille du Midi at
12,606 ft. (3842 m.).

To Courmayeur
Pte. Helbronner
3462m. Italy

Vallée Blanche

Aiguille du Midi
3842m.

Lac Bleu 2299m.

Start and End of Walk
Plan de l'Aiguille
2310m.

Chamonix 1036m.

Take the giant cable car up to the mid-station at 7579
ft. (2310 m.) and continue to the Aiguille du Midi. After exiting, cross the footbridge, walking to your right to visit the
Mont Blanc Terrace. After appreciating the fabulous views
of Mont Blanc, you might wish to take the elevator to Galerie
du Mont Blanc at the summit. When ready, return to the
footbridge, following the signs to Galerie de la Vallée
Blanche that lead you to the Helbronner Gondola and the
ice tunnel. Make sure you walk into the ice tunnel and on to
the little ledge. If you are lucky you will see climbers coming
out of the clouds after traversing the mountain below you.

☞ **HINT: Even on a hot, summer day this station is often
well below freezing. Stow your insulated jacket in
your backpack along with sunglasses and sunscreen.**

Follow the signs to Helbronner for the 40-minute ride over the glacier in a small gondola. A round trip and visit from the Aiguille can last as long as three hours, with a 20-minute ride down from the Aiguille peak to return to Chamonix. If you choose to do so, it's another 40 minutes down to the Courmayeur lift station, situated on the outskirts of town, but it is recommended that a visit to Courmayeur be left for another day.

When ready to return, follow the green "Chamonix" signs to the cable car departure. On very busy days, boarding passes are distributed for the descent. You may pick them up on your arrival at the information desk at the footbridge, specifying the time you would like to return.

> ☞ **HINT: The altitude may create dizziness or headaches. Walk slowly and rest often until you adjust. If you find you are not able to talk or walk without being out of breath, you might wish to leave early.**

Return to the mid-station at Plan de l'Aiguille for a 30-minute walk to Lac Bleu, on an open, rocky trail. You should leave about and one and one-quarter hours for the well-signed, round-trip walk and visit. When ready, descend to Chamonix by cable car from Plan de l'Aiguille.

Walk #5: Chamonix on Petit Balcon Sud to Les Tines to Les Praz to Chamonix

Walking Easy Time
3 hours

The walk on the Petit Balcon Sud proceeds in an easterly direction through the forest at about 3937 ft. (1200 m.). It is an enjoyable walk for a cloudy day because the trail is never very far from the valley floor, in case of inclement weather. The most challenging part of today's walk takes place in the first 45 minutes, when *Easy Walkers* will ascend from 3379 ft. (1030 m.) to 3953 ft. (1205 m.), a rise of 575 ft. (175 m.). The path is wide and rocky and climbs to reach the Petit Balcon Sud trail above les Nantes, overlooking the Chamonix golf course, where it then descends gradually to 3583 ft. (1092 m.). The return to Chamonix is on a well-engineered, level path along the l'Arve River, adjacent to the golf course, walking to les Praz and into Chamonix.

Start: Pack a picnic today and start your walk from the Hotel Sapinière. Turn right immediately and walk to the end of the street, then turn left. After a few minutes you will see a marked path on the right ascending to Petit Balcon Sud. This path is easily followed, but rises steadily for about 45 minutes. *Easy Walkers* should set a slow but comfortable pace and stop as needed.

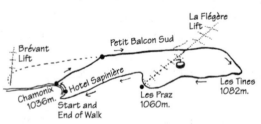

Once on the Petit Balcon Sud, proceed to your lower right in the direction of Chalet de la Floria, still mostly through the forest. After another 15 minutes, the road forks again. This time you will walk to the right, **not** following the ascending path to the left to the Chalet de la Floria, but continuing on the Petit Balcon Sud. As you walk you can look down on the Chamonix golf course and the path you will take on your return to Chamonix.

The trail continues to descend from 3937 ft. (1200 m.) to 3557 ft. (1084 m.), bordered with blueberries and wild strawberries (*frais de bois*)—a delicious snack if ripe. Continue in the direction of les Tines and Pont de la Forge. This path ends within a few minutes at the bridge over the Arve River, where a gentle trail runs in both directions along the river. Turn right in the direction of le Paradis for the return to Chamonix. This is a level walking path through the forest with several nice picnic areas on your right and flowing streams from the Arve River on your left.

After about 1000 ft. (300 m.) you will come to a small pathside restaurant with cabins and the recreation area les Paradis des Praz. Within a few minutes you'll reach the closed gates of the Chamonix golf course. Follow the path around to your left and over the river, turning right again on this flat walking path. On your left is the entry to the driving range. Since you won't have your golf clubs with you today, continue to walk through the Chamonix golf course parking area to the auto road, passing the very pretty Labrador Hotel. Turn right on the road for a few minutes, following signs to la Flégère cable station. Make a right turn into the parking lot, walk past the station, cross over the river and turn left in the direction of the sign pointing to Chamonix. This path takes you into Chamonix in 30 minutes.

Walk #6: Prarion to Col de Voza, Excursion to Nid d'Aigle with Glacier Visit, Return to Les Houches, Excursion to Les Bossons Glacier, Walk to Chamonix

Walking Easy Time
2½ to 3½ hours

Easy Walkers will use many kinds of transportation to accomplish today's exciting walks and excursions. Allow most of the day for this outing. You will depart from Chamonix by bus for a short ride to les Houches and a gondola ride to Prarion. A short, downhill walk leads you to Col de Voza where you will board the Mont Blanc Tramway for an exciting mountain train ride up to Nid d'Aigle at 7783 ft. (2372 m.), with views over the Glacier de Bionnassay. A somewhat steep, rocky descent is available for a closer look at the glacier. You will meet climbers in full mountain regalia coming from and going to the *refuges* in the area, located between 9300 and 13,125 ft. (3000 and 4000 m.).

After a short visit you will return by tram to its first stop at Bellevue, where you will take the Bellevue/St. Gervais cable car down to les Houches. Your next visit, after a short bus ride, will be to the imposing Bossons glacier for a chairlift ride up to its leading edge. A walk back to Chamonix along the valley floor completes a very full and gratifying day.

Directions: After picking up your picnic provisions, walk to the central Chamonix bus station next to the Tourist Office and purchase a round-trip ticket to les Houches. Take the 9:00 am bus for the 20-minute ride through les Bossons, where you will return later for the chairlift ride to the glacier, and exit the bus at the

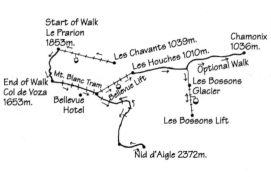

last stop in les Houches/les Chavants. Purchase a one-way ticket and take the short gondola ride up to le Prarion at 6080 ft. (1853 m.).

Start: Walk up the hill past le Prarion Hotel and Café, following the signed directions to Col de Voza. Turn left and walk down the wide trail for a 25-minute descent to Col de Voza at 5424 ft. (1653 m.). This path takes you directly to the Tramway du Mont Blanc station. Purchase a ticket to Nid d'Aigle with a return to Bellevue. You should plan on taking the 10:50 am train, bringing you to the glacier at 11:20 am. You must make reservations for the return trip IMMEDIATELY upon arriving at the glacier in order to make sure of your return time, based on the popularity of this scenic spot. Plan to take the 12:30 pm tram back to Bellevue, arriving at 12:50 pm.

    ☞ **HINT: For best views, try to sit on the right side of the tram going to the glacier.**

The Bellevue cable car is a short walk up the meadow to your right and is in the building in front of a small restaurant. The cable car is closed for lunch between 12:30 and 1:30 pm, so it might be a good idea to picnic in the pleasant meadows until it is time to catch the 1:30 pm car down to les Houches. Purchase a one-way ticket for the short ride down the mountain. If you are lucky, the 1:30 pm Chamonix bus to les Bossons will be a few minutes late—if it has already departed, walk to your right along the road into the little village of les Houches to explore the shops while waiting for the 2:30 pm Chamonix bus. Tell the driver you wish to get off at les Bossons chairlift and he will stamp your bus ticket accordingly and let you off in the parking area of les Bossons lift station.

Purchase a round-trip ticket for the exciting chairlift ride to the edge of the Bossons glacier, which dominates the entire Chamonix valley. After visiting the glacier and returning to the parking area, you have two options, depending on the time and your attitude. You can walk down to the main auto road, crossing under the railroad tracks and taking a right turn on the path past les Pelerins and Lacs des Gail-lands—walking into Chamonix. Or, if you wish, wait for the Chamonix bus.

Walk #7: Le Tour Lift to Top Station, Walk to Col de Balme to Col des Posettes to Charamillon Mid-Station to Le Tour

 Walking Easy Time
2½ to 3½ hours

The visit to Col de Balme is not only one of the highlights of a visit to Chamonix, but truly stands on its own as one of our all-time favorite day hikes. The tiny, ancient hamlet of le Tour is situated at one end of the Chamonix valley, sur-rounded by high, grassy meadows and framed by snow-cov-ered peaks. *Easy Walkers* will leave Chamonix by public bus for a 20-minute ride to le Tour lift station, which in the winter services 2000 skiers a day. The 14-minute trip to the top at 7153 ft. (2180 m.) is interrupted only by a quick change at the mid-station from a six-person gondola to a four-place open chairlift.

The walk begins at the top station in the direction of Col de Balme to the Hotel Suisse on the Swiss border with France. Many walkers continue on into Switzerland, but to-day *Easy Walkers* will hike along the perimeter of the "punchbowl" around le Tour to Col des Posettes and even-tually back to the Charamillon Mid-Station at 6070 ft. (1850 m.), with a final descent to le Tour at 4767 ft. (1453 m.). The views are stunning in all directions, and the Mont Blanc massif takes on a new perspective from the northeast—on a clear day *Easy Walkers* will be able to see throughout the Chamonix valley. Remember to pack a sweatshirt along with lunch—it can be cool at the top.

Directions: Take the 9:30 or 10:30 am bus to le Tour lift station. Buy a one-way ticket to Col de Balme top station, where the walk begins. The first stage of the lift is a continuously moving six-person gondola, and you transfer immediately from it to the four-seat chairlift for a final ascent to the top station.

Start: Follow signs to Col de Balme on a gently ascending path for the 15-minute walk to the hotel. You are now at the Swiss border, easily recognized by the friendly and familiar yellow signs directing hikers to various Swiss locations. Take enough time to view the panorama as it unfolds before you—this is one of the most beautiful sites on any walking itinerary. (It's a good idea to stop walk-

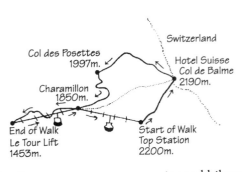

ing when you admire the scenery—even experienced hikers have been known to trip over a stray rock in the path and this is no time to damage an ankle or toe.)

When ready, follow signs to Col des Posettes, which, incidentally, is part of the Mont Blanc Trail (TMB). As you look to your left you will see your destination and the path you'll be walking on. The comfortable trail winds around a grassy mountain, clearly marked before it descends to Col des Posettes. The snow-covered Mont Blanc massif towers over the Chamonix valley in front of you as you walk along the well-defined path on the perimeter of this mountain, with colorful wildflowers all around and cowbells clanging in the *alpe* below. You will reach a wide path and a group of signs that take you left, in the direction of the Charamillon mid-station, where the path continues to descend to le Tour. Stay on the wide, jeep path as it switches back and forth to le Tour lift station.

> ☞ **HINT: This path descends from the mid-station at 6070 ft. (1850 m.) to le Tour at 4767 ft. (1453 m.). If you feel that this descent of 1303 ft. (397 m.) in an hour may be too much for your knees, take the gondola down from the mid-station.**

Buses leave for Chamonix from le Tour lift station (where you were dropped off in the morning), every half-hour from 2:30 pm to 5:30 pm. You might enjoy a stroll through the old hamlet of le Tour, cut off in the past from the rest of the Chamonix valley by heavy snows and avalanches—today a prominent ski center with seven ski lifts, 14 ski runs, numerous cross-country trails and over 2000 skiers a day taking advantage of this winter wonderland.

Walk #8: Excursion to L'Index, Walk La Flégère to Argentière

Walking Easy Time
2½ hours

After a visit by chairlift to l'Index at 7825 ft. (2385 m.) to see summer skiers and fabulous views of the Aiguilles Rouges, you will walk on a pleasant, descending trail from the la Flégère lift station to the busy little village of Argentière.

The trail is situated at a level between the Grand Balcon Sud, part of the Trail du Mont Blanc (TMB), and the Petit Balcon Sud, site of a walk on another day (see Walk #5). *Easy Walkers* will leave from Chalet de la Flégère at 6158 ft. (1877 m.) and finish the walk in Argentière at 4102 ft. (1250 m.), with a bus trip back to Chamonix.

Directions: Take the bus to the Flégère lift at les Praz, or follow the gentle, 30-minute walk from Chamonix along the river, directly to the Flégère lift station. If you decide to walk, leave Chamonix and walk down the little street in front of the hospital (av. de la Plage). It takes you over a small bridge across the Arve River. Turn immediately left, picking up a pleasant walking path leading directly into the lift station. Buy a lift ticket to l'Index with a return to la Flégère. Take the large cable car to la Flégère and walk up to the chairlift that runs continuously to

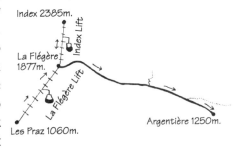

l'Index. You will probably see summer skiers on the slopes under the impressive Aiguilles Rouges. When ready, return to la Flégère by chairlift.

Start: Pick up the trail in back of the restaurant, and after crossing under a small ski lift, take the right fork in the direction of Argentière. This walk is largely through the forest, with little chance of distraction except for two intervening paths on your left, one at 4984 ft. (1519 m.) bringing climbers up to the Chalet des Chéserys. Continue on the main path, resisting another path at 4715 ft. (1437 m.) which climbs up the mountain. Continue down in the signed direction of Argentière at 4101 ft. (1250 m.), entering directly into this busy village. Locate the bus stop on the main auto road in the village center for the ride back to Chamonix.

Aggressive walkers have the option of walking west on the main village street in the direction of Chamonix, picking up the Petit Balcon Sud and walking into les Tines. There you may follow the easy, low path to le Paradis, staying left of the Chamonix Golf Course and the Labrador Hotel, into les Praz and la Flégère lift station you were at this morning. Pick up the Chamonix walk in back of the lift station. At any one of these major points you can also take the Chamonix bus to return.

MEGÈVE

Lovely Megève is in Pays du Mont Blanc (Mont Blanc Country), one of 14 villages and 400 hamlets in the shadow of the impressive 15,772-foot (4807-meter) Mont Blanc peak, bordered by the Valais region of Switzerland and Italy's Aosta Valley. The origin of the name Megève can be found in the ancient Celtic language: *mag* (village) and *eva* (water), referring to the village's position between two rivers. A charming village of 4900 friendly inhabitants, Megève is built on narrow, cobblestone streets, with an imposing, 14th-century church towering over many ancient buildings.

Proudly traditional in terms of architecture and culture, one doesn't have to go far to find all the conveniences and luxuries of modern life. In fact, Megève is one of the more sophisticated mountain villages in the French Alps, with chic boutiques and sports, relaxation and fitness centers everywhere. Lodgings range from four-star luxury hotels to rental apartments and *gites*, simple farmhouse accommodations. The active and easily accessible Megève Tourist Office is located in a remarkably beautiful, landmark building just off the pedestrian-only street in the village center and has a well-informed and courteous staff, helpful in finding suitable accommodations as well as providing hiking maps and walking information. At night, the small bridges over the river are attractively lit, and crowded pedestrian streets and outdoor cafés are filled with vacationers enjoying a coffee or ice cream.

There are over 90 miles (150 km) of hiking trails at all levels in the Megève area, many on mountain paths facing the Mont Blanc range, others winding past local farms and barns, or through shaded pine forests and flower-filled meadows. Megève's high valleys are covered with pine, larch, and willow trees, while the valley floor is lined with maple, ash and birch. The scenery is a tranquil contrast of verdant, green valleys, colorful, flower-filled hillsides and snow-capped mountains, home to chamois, ibex and marmot.

Three major lifts are available to walkers in Megève in summer: Mont d'Arbois at 6027 ft. (1837 m.), Rochebrune at 5784 ft. (1763 m.), and Jaillet at 5200 ft. (1585 m.), leading to a variety of high-altitude, scenic day-hikes, with stops at country inns and restaurants along the way. Local mini-buses (*navettes*) operate reasonably frequently from the modern, centrally located bus terminal, and they provide inexpensive and direct transportation between July and September to cable cars, gondolas and chairlifts at the start or finish of many *Walking Easy* hikes.

Megève is well located, only a short distance from the internationally famous resort of Chamonix (another *Easy Walker* base village), and it is surrounded by charming small villages and hamlets. Excursions to Chamonix, Annecy, Lake Geneva, Grenoble, Albertville and the Aosta Valley in Italy are easily accomplished, as SAT intercity buses also operate from Megève.

Megève hosts sports contests and music concerts, both classical and jazz, and offers many options for walking, sightseeing, or spending a relaxing evening in town. The authors were fortunate to be in Megève over the second week of July during Bastille Day festivities. Megève celebrated with their First Annual New Orleans Jazz Contest, inviting 15 outstanding jazz groups from England, Switzerland, Belgium and France. They performed on stages erected around the village, as judges evaluated and spectators jammed the streets enjoying the entertainment. The winner was invited to perform at the Annual Megève Jazz Festival in August.

Megève is an upbeat village—good food, good wine, good accommodations, good entertainment, nice people, a helpful Tourist Office and, most important for *Easy Walkers*, good walking.

Transportation to Megève

By Plane: Geneva-Cointrin International Airport is 43 miles (70 km) from Megève. The airport has regular train service to Sallanches 7 miles (12 kms) away, with a bus connection to Megève. In summer there is only one bus a day to and from the Geneva airport to Megève, but many car rental agencies are also located at the airport. Charles de Gaulle Airport is also an option for those who'll be spending time in Paris as well.

Sample Timetable

Dep. Geneva Airport	4:10 pm (train)
Dep. Geneva Train Station	4:30 pm (bus)
Arr. Megève	6:40 pm
Dep. Megève	7:00 am (bus)
Dep. Geneva Train Station	9:30 am (train)
Arr. Geneva Airport	9:45 am

By Car: At 372 miles (600 km), the most direct auto route from Paris to Megève is to drive from Paris to Mâcon on A6, picking up A40 around Bourg-en-Bresse and staying on A40 around Geneva east towards Chamonix. At Sallanches, take N212 south into Megève. (For directions from Paris' Charles de Gaulle Airport, please see the "Chamonix" chapter's Transportation section.)

By Train: Railroad stations for the TGV high-speed trains of the SNCF (French Railways) are in Sallanches or at the St. Gervais/Le Fayet terminal, about a half-hour drive from

Megève. Night and day trains are available, as well as first- and second-class sleeping cars to and from Paris. A 30-minute bus ride connects Megève to arriving trains.

By Bus: The Société Alpine Transporte Company (SAT) operates local buses from the Megève bus station, located on main road N212, in front of the Sports Center. They run to and from Combloux, Saint-Gervais, Le Fayet, Sallanches and Chamonix in one direction and Praz sur Arly, Flumet, Ugine, Albertville and Annecy in the opposite direction. Buses also operate once a day to and from Geneva and once a day between Megève and Grenoble. Check at the information counter in the bus terminal for current schedules.

Sample Bus Schedules

Dep. Megève	8:10 am
Dep. Praz sur Arly	8:20 am
Dep. Flumet	8:30 am
Dep. Ugine	8:55 am
Arr. Annecy	9:45 am

Local Megève Bus Service (*Navettes*): In summer, local buses run from the Megève Bus Station on Route N212, next to the Hotel Grange D'Arly and in front of the Sports Center, to Mont d'Arbois Cable Station and Cote 2000, with another line going to Rochebrune Cable Station and Faucigny. The fare is 8, 13 or 19 FF for a one-way trip, depending on your destination, but ten-trip discount cards are available. Check at the Tourist Office or bus station for current schedules and fares.

Sample *Navette* Schedules

Dep. Megève Bus Terminal	9:00 am
Arr. Mont d'Arbois Lift	9:10 am
Dep. Megève Bus Terminal	9:30 am
Arr. Rochebrune Lift	9:40 am

Activities in Megève

This section lists activities available in Megève on days when additions or alternatives to walking are desired. The Megève Tourist Office is located in its new quarters in the restored Maison des Frères, on the walking street in the center of Megève, tel: 50-21-27-28.

Bison-breeding Farm - This unusual mountain farm, in the heart of a chamois reserve under the peak of Mont-Joly, is now reserved for breeding a herd of bison. For more information about visits, tel: 50-91-86-60.

Carriage Rides - A picturesque tradition and an enjoyable way to see the Megève area is to go by horse carriage. They are located outside the church square and cost from 60 to 210 FF per ride.

Casino - The casino is on Place de la Résistance and is open every day at 5:00 pm to play *boule*.

Churches - Originally built by Benedictine monks in 1085, the **St. Jean-Baptiste Church** has a long and interesting history. The choir loft was raised at the end of the 14th century; the nave dates from 1692; and the gilded Virgin and Romanesque-style bell tower dates from 1754. The vaults were painted in 1828, and the newest section, the Stations of the Cross, was created in 1956. Built in the mid-1800s and inspired by the Way of the Cross, or Golgotha, the **Cavalry of Megève** is on the eastern outskirts of Megève. There are 14 chapels tracing scenes of Christ's Passion in wooden Baroque, Rococo and Tuscan figures.

Concerts - A folk group representing the Savoyard heritage of the area, **Mailles et Béguines** revives old music, song, dance and costumes. *Mailles*, men's geometrically embroidered wool jackets, and *béguines*, women's tulle headpieces, gave rise to the name. Check with the Tourist Office for performance dates, usually on a holiday such as Bastille Day. Other musical events include the Megève Jazz Contest, with international bands playing authentic New Orleans jazz, the International Musical Meetings with classical concerts and master classes, and the Annual Megève Jazz Festival featuring New Orleans, be-bop and modern styles.

Festivals - There is a horse festival, celebrating local folklore with costumes of the past, and the Sainte Croix Fair in September, exhibiting the agricultural activity still performed by the 100 area farms and announcing the return of the cattle from high mountain pastures.

Fishing - Licenses are available at the Tourist Office.

Fitness Parcours (Trim Trail) - At Mont d'Arbois/Cote 2000, at an altitude of 4922 ft. (1500 m.), there is fitness equipment laid out on a forest trail.

Golf - The 18-hole, par 72, Mont d'Arbois golf course is on a sunny, tree-filled plateau, with breathtaking views and the Aiguilles de Warens and Aravis mountains as a backdrop. A driving range and putting green are also available. For information and reservations, tel: 50-21-29-79.

Horseback Riding - A riding ring is available at le Manoir riding club at le Maz, tel: 50-21-31-77. Horseback riding and trekking can be found at les Coudrettes Riding Centre located near the Rochebrune cable car, tel: 50-21-16-52; at Ranch de la Daylle at les Perchets, tel: 50-58-77-12; and at Mont d'Arbois Riding Club in le Maz, tel: 50-21-31-77.

Ice Skating - The indoor Olympic ice rink at the Sports and Congress Centre is 60 x 30 meters, tel: 50-93-01-01.

Market - In summer, an outdoor market is held every Friday in the parking area in front of the Sports and Congress

Centre. It features local cheeses and sausages, fresh produce grown in the area, and clothing stalls.

Miniature Golf - For information call the Sports and Congress Centre at 50-93-01-01.

Mountain Biking - Mountain bikes can be used on signed paths, across meadows and pastures, through cool forests, around peaceful villages. Check with the Tourist Office for maps and rentals.

Museums - A former home, the **Megève Museum** is located at 66, rue Comte de Capré, and is open Monday to Saturday from 3:00 pm to 7:00 pm; exhibits change periodically. Located at 88, rue du Vieux Marché in an old farmhouse, the **Haute Val d'Arly Museum** is open daily from 3:00 to 6:30 pm and Wednesday evenings; its exhibits depict the local Savoie heritage with farming, crafts, skiing, and mountaineering exhibits.

Paragliding - Megève Parapente is licensed to give introductory to advanced courses, tel: 50-58-90-64.

Plane Rides - Aèro-Cime offers tourist flights over Mont Blanc, tel: 50-21-33-67. Club des Sports has "discovery" flights in a two-seater plane, tel: 50-21-31-50.

Sports Events - The La Megève-Mont Blanc bicycle race crosses five difficult passes with a height difference of 11,766 ft. (3586 m.) and a total length of 93 miles (150 kms).

Summer Sledge - This long course is at the Prellet ski lift, located next to the Jaillet cable car, and consists of two 1641-foot-long (500 m.) tracks with a drop of 328 ft. (100 m.), traversed in a miniature luge. It is open every day from 10:00 am to 12:30 pm and 2:00 pm to 6:30 pm, and Tuesday and Friday from 8:30 pm to 10:30 pm as well.

Swimming - There is an outdoor, heated Olympic-sized pool and an indoor heated pool available to visitors at the fabulous Sports and Congress Centre (Palais des Sports et des Congrès), located in back of the town bus terminal on the main road. For information call 50-93-01-01.

Tennis - There are seven courts and two training walls at the Mt-d'Arbois Tennis Club, tel: 50-21-31-51 for costs and reservations. 15 outdoor courts are available, including two clay and three lighted at the Sports and Congress Centre, tel: 50-93-01-01.

Excursions in and around Megève

This section introduces day excursions that *Easy Walkers* will enjoy when an alternative to walking is desired. Be sure to check current timetables for best connections if public transportation is used.

1. Lifts in and around Megève

A) Téléphérique de Rochebrune - This cable car rises to 5752 ft. (1753 m.) in about five minutes. It is open every day from 9:00 am to 1:00 pm and 2:00 pm to 6:00 pm, leaving every half-hour. (See Walks #2 and #7 for more details.)
  Directions: Take the local bus from the bus station next to the Hotel Grange d'Arly.

B) Télécabine Mont d'Arbois - The gondola rises to 5978 ft. (1822 m.) and is open every day from 9:00 am to 6:00 pm, leaving every half hour. (See Walks #3 and #5 for more details.)
  Directions: Take the local bus from the bus station next to the Hotel Grange d'Arly.

C) Télécabine du Jaillet - Rising to 5204 ft. (1586 m.), the gondola runs every day from 9:15 am to 1:00 pm and from 2:00 pm to 6:00 pm. The top station provides fabulous views of the snow-covered Mont Blanc range, towering over the green hills around Megève. (See Walks #1 and #4 for more details.)

Directions: Walk on the street to the right of the Sports Center, up the hill, following the sign to Jaillet marked *pietons* (walkers).

2. Chamonix - This world capital of mountaineering is dominated by the majesty of Mont Blanc, the highest mountain in Europe, and two imposing glaciers, Mer de Glace and les Bossons, but the town successfully combines the boutiques, restaurants, hotels and services of a large resort with the awesome natural surroundings of the surrounding Alps. (See the "Chamonix" chapter for more details.)

Directions: By car - Take N212 north, following signs through St. Gervais to Chamonix. Reverse directions to return. By bus - The 8:30 am bus from Megève arrives in Chamonix at 9:25 am. It leaves for the return at 6:05 pm, arriving in Megève at 7:40 pm. Or, you can take an SAT excursion to Chamonix and the Chamonix valley, leaving every Saturday.

3. Evian-les-Bains - See the "Chamonix" chapter, Excursion #2.

Directions: By car - Follow N212 north to N205 into Cluses, then take D902 to Thonon and drive east on N5 to Evian. Return on a circle route by driving west on N5 to Thonon, then taking D903 to N206 to Annemosse. Pick up N205 to Sallanches and N212 into Megève.

☞ **HINT: Remember your passport if you are leaving France on this or any other excursion!**

4. Annecy - See the "Chamonix" chapter, Excursion #4.

Directions: By car - Drive south on N212 to Aciéries, picking up N508 towards Ugine. Drive through Faverges and continue around the left side of the lake to Annecy. By bus - The 8:10 am bus from Megève arrives in Annecy at 9:45 am. To return, take the 3:00 pm bus, arriving in Megève at 4:40 pm. Or, you can take a SAT excursion bus to Annecy, leaving every Saturday.

5. Albertville - Of interest here is the **XVI Winter Olympic Games Visitors Center**, an exhibition and information area where you can relive the atmosphere of the 1992 Olympics. Note the costumes from the opening and closing ceremonies, as well as photos and films. The center is open daily (except Sunday) from 9:00 am to 7:00 pm, and admission is free.

On a hill just above Albertville is the medieval city of **Conflans**, with its ancient wrought-iron signs and 12th- to 13th-century facades, surrounded by ancient ramparts. Take time to look at the **castle** and walk on the old, winding streets of Conflans. You enter the town through a gateway, **la Porte de Savoie**, with remains of the town walls rebuilt in the 14th century still visible. Opposite the gate is **la Tour Ramus**, a 15th-century tower containing only a staircase. Walking further, you will see a little square with a **stone fountain**, designed in 1711 by an officer in the army of King Louis XIV of France.

On Rue Gabriel Pérouse, a little path leads to **la Place de la Petite Roche** (Little Rock Square), where strong arches still support the walls. The old shop district is located from here to the main square, **la Grande Place**. To the left, a short, steep flight of stairs leads to the **church**, built in the 18th century on the site of a church burned in 1632. Note the 1714 altarpiece and the Baroque pulpit. If you walk up the path at the church, the highest point in the area is at the ruins of the Red Castle, or **le Château Rouge**, built in the 14th century, now in complete disrepair. Walk back and pass through **la Porte Tarine** or the Tarin Gate, used by ancient peoples coming from the Tarentaise region and from Italy. Two brick arches can still be seen.

If you return to la Grand Place, the main square where markets and fairs were held for centuries, note the fountain in the middle, designed in Baroque style in 1750. Also in the square is the Red House, **la Maison Rouge**, built in 1397 and now used as a museum of local history and ethnology of the Savoy. In la Place de la Grande Roche is the **Saracen tower**, built in the 12th century. Wander in the maze of narrow, cobblestone streets where old houses have been converted to cafés and workshops.

Directions: By car - Take N212 southwest to Albertville. By bus - The 12:50 pm bus arrives in Albertville at 1:45 pm. To return, take the 5:00 pm bus, arriving in Megève at 6:00 pm. Or, you can take a SAT excursion bus.

6. Montreux, Switzerland - See the "Chamonix" chapter, Excursion #6.

Directions: By car - Drive on N212 north past St. Gervais, following signs to Chamonix. Then take 506 east past Chamonix, over the Swiss border, through Col de la Forclaz to Martigny and highway N9 into Montreux (following the signs to Lausanne). Or, you can take a full day's excursion to Gruyère and Montreux by SAT bus.

7. Lausanne, Switzerland - See the "Chamonix" chapter, Excursion #6.

Directions: By car - Take N212 north to St. Gervais. Drive east, following signs to Chamonix, then over the Swiss border and through Col de la Forclaz to Martigny. Pick up highway N9, driving past Montreux and Vevey, around Lake Geneva into Lausanne.

8. Aosta, Italy - See the "Chamonix" chapter, Excursion #9.

Directions: By car - Take N212 north through St. Gervais, following signs to Chamonix. Drive through the Mont Blanc Tunnel on S26, continuing east into Aosta on the same road. By bus - Every Thursday a SAT excursion bus leaves for Aosta. Every Tuesday an excursion bus goes to Aosta and Cogne, in Gran Paradiso Park.

9. Courmayeur, Italy - See the "Chamonix" chapter, Excursion #7.

Directions: By car - Take N212 north to St. Gervais, following signs to Chamonix. Drive through the Tunnel du Mont Blanc, continuing into Courmayeur.

10. Geneva, Switzerland - See the "Chamonix" chapter, Excursion #10.

Directions: By car - Take N212 north out of Megève to N205 into Geneva. By bus - SAT excursions can take you to and from Geneva every Friday.

11. The Société Alpes Transports - The SAT bus station and information office is located next to the Hotel Grange d'Arly, in front of the Sports Center on the main route through town, tel: 50-21-25-18. This company runs the following bus excursions in summer: Col des Saisies/Beaufort, Barrage D'Emosson, les Lindarets, Annecy, Aoste/Cogne, Yvoire, Fer à Cheval, le Val D'Anniviers, Cordon et son Goûter, Aoste, Zermatt, Geneva, Aravis/Colombiere, Tour du Mont-Blanc/Grand Saint Bernard Hospice/Aosta Valley, Vallée de Chamonix, Annecy, Canal de Savieres, le Pays Rochois, Rive Suisse du Léman, le Lac Majeur, les Glaciers du Rhone, Gruyère/Montreux, Conflans/Albertville, Lac de Champex, le Lac Vert, and Venice.

C. Lipton

Above: French Alps in July

Below: Trail and Glacier at Nid d'Aigle

C. Lipton

C. Lipton

Above: Mer de Glace

Below: Trail to Col des Posettes in the Chamonix Valley

C. Lipton

C. Lipton

Above: Mont Blanc overlooking Lac Marlou

Below: Réallon from Fortress Trail near Embrun

C. Lipton

Above: Typical Mountain Trail in the French Alps

Below: Refuge du Saut in Vanoise National Park

Megève Walks

Recommended Map: Carte des Promenades, Megève

Walk #1: Introductory Walk - Lift to Le Jaillet, Walk to Chalet de la Vieille to Odier to Megève

Walking Easy Time
2½ hours

This lovely ramble is a good introduction to walking in the heights around Megève. If you arrive in Megève in the morning, it is the kind of walk you might wish to take after settling into your hotel—not particularly demanding or long. You will take the Jaillet gondola up to the top station and walk to Chalet de la Vieille on a lovely path with sensational views of the snow-covered Mont Blanc range, a stunning backdrop to the green, rolling hills around Megève. Along the way you can visit a charming mountain restaurant (with sun terrace) overlooking the valley and Mont Blanc. At Chalet de la Vieille, you will turn down the mountain to return to Megève through the suburban community of Odier.

Directions: Facing the bus station on the main road, walk to your right, turning left up the hill, and proceed past the Palais de Sport, in the direction of le Jaillet. Make a right turn, following the sign "Télécabine du Jaillet - Pietons." This short, uphill walk brings you to the lift entrance. Purchase a one-way ticket to the top; if over 60, ask for a senior discount. The modern, six-person gondolas move only on the hour and half-hour for the seven-minute ride, taking all passengers up at those times.

Start: The top station is at 5200 ft. (1585 m.) with a restaurant and facilities. Walk straight ahead for only a minute to a sign that directs you to the right on path R3. The wide, comfortable path descends gently under a ski lift, leading *Easy Walkers* to the little mountain restaurant, la Ravine, on the right, with marvelous views from its sun terrace. Pause a while and enjoy the spectacular scenery of the snow-covered Mont Blanc range in the distance. You might sample the homemade blueberry torte, with the sound

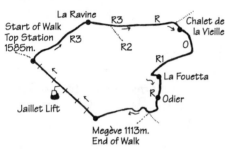

of cowbells clanging gently in the meadow. This seems to be a favorite spot of visiting French families.

When ready, continue ahead on R3. Do **not** turn down the mountain on R2 to la Fouetta, but continue ahead on R3 in the direction of Beauregard and Chalet de la Vieille. Turn sharply right on a path signed only "Chalet de la Vieille," this short descent taking you to the old barn at the chalet. Walk left of the chalet, a small restaurant with a great view and facilities, and turn right at signed path O, in the direction of Vauvray. This typical narrow mountain path descends through forests and meadows, ending at an auto road with a small parking area.

Turn right on this road, R1, in the direction of Megève, and continue to another small parking area marked "La Fouetta." Look for the sign "R" in the parking area, leading to Odier. This mountain trail descends again, but it can be wet at times—walk carefully. You will soon be in Odier. Turn left on the small road, meeting a major auto road where you will turn right. Make your first right turn again and walk up the road. Turn left at an unmarked, grassy wagon path with an orange pump, winding through the meadow and coming out on another auto road. Turn left, then right, and within a few minutes you will be at le Jaillet where you started this morning. A quick walk past the sports center and the bus station brings you back to your hotel.

Walk #2: Lift to Rochebrune, Walk to L'Alpette to Les Lanchettes to Les Jardins to Javen to Le Maz to Megève

Walking Easy Time
3½ hours

Our walk today begins at the top station of the Rochebrune cable lift (Téléphérique du Rochebrune), a starting point for many walks as well as a jumping-off place for paragliders. You will walk up to l'Alpette Restaurant, a rise of 355 ft. (108 m.), and continue gently downhill to the cutoff trail to les Lanchettes. This trail affords views of the Aiguille Croche, the Tête de la Combaz and Mont Joly, as well as part of the Mont Blanc massif. The remainder of the hike descends through Javen, with a visit to the tiny hamlet of le Maz for the final descent into the center of Megève. The walking is mostly downhill, except for the first 35-minute ascent to l'Alpette from Rochebrune. If you haven't packed a picnic lunch, there are several restaurants with facilities along the way.

 HINT: When walking uphill, lean slightly forward, take consistent, slow strides, and rest as needed. When walking downhill, lean slightly backwards with

knees slightly bent, taking small steps and turning from side to side as you descend.

Directions: Take the 9:30 am bus at the bus stop next to the Hotel Grange d'Arly, for the ten-minute ride to the Rochebrune Lift Station. Or, if you wish, it is a 20-minute walk up the hill to the cable station. Purchase a one-way lift ticket to Rochebrune at 5755 ft. (1754 m.) for the five-minute ascent. If applicable, ask for a senior discount.

Start: The Megève Tourist Office has marked the routes and corresponding walking map simply and clearly, using easy-to-follow coding so there is no chance for confusion. Follow the G route to l'Alpette for a 35-minute ascent, continuing around until you see a sign indicating the upcoming restaurant (with a nice view, sun terrace and facilities).

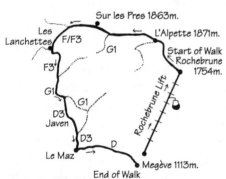

When ready, walk back to the main path and follow the sign for F/G. After a few minutes you'll pass a small, mountain farm (Sur les Pres) serving homemade sausages, local cheese and cold drinks, with the sound of cowbells gently clanging an accompaniment to the lovely views. In about 30 minutes you will turn left on F/F3, descending towards les Lanchettes. Continue down on F3, which eventually turns into G1. Stay right, taking D3 in the direction of Javen at 4472 ft. (1363 m.). As you descend you will pass over grassy meadows and through pine forests on a wide jeep trail.

On occasion you will come across a wire fence crossing the trail, placed there to keep the cows in the meadow. Unhook the wire, remembering to snap it back to reattach—this occurs twice as you walk down the mountain. The little mountain *altiport* is on your right and the village of Megève on the left. Make sure you remain on D3, and you will soon approach an auto road. Turn right on this road and walk a few minutes until, on the right, you see an old church with its lovely clock. This is the quaint hamlet of le Maz. Turn left on the road opposite the church, marked "D" on your map but not on the path, with a sign pointing to Megève. This path continues down, through farms and then forest, directly into the center of Megève.

Walk #3: Lift to Mont d'Arbois, Walk to Mont Joux to Hermance to Le Planay to Le Maz to Megève

Walking Easy Time
4 hours

This popular Mont d'Arbois hike is rated "more challenging," not because of any particular difficulty of the trail, but because of its long ascents and descents. The paths are easily found and well-marked—Megève continues to do a particularly good job of keying trails to its walking map. While there are numerous rest and restaurant stops on top of Mont d'Arbois, there are none on the descending trails between Pavillon du Mont Joly and Megève, so it might be a good idea to pack a picnic lunch and, of course, the ever-necessary bottle of water.

Walkers will have immediate ascents and descents after leaving the lift, and will head towards Mont Joly with the trail rising from 5985 ft. (1824 m.) to 6496 ft. (1980 m.) before descending to le Planay. (For those of you who are interested in that ascent to Mont Joly at 8285 ft. (2525 m.), the trail is well-marked and well-traveled.) The descent to le Planay passes through the ancient hamlet of Hermance, ducking in and out of shady forests and flower-filled meadows. At le Planay, a good picnic spot, you will begin the return to Megève with a short walk along the road and a final descent through the picturesque hamlet of le Maz.

Directions: Take the 10:15 am *navette* from the bus station next to the Hotel Grange d'Arly for the ten-minute ride to the Mont d'Arbois lift station. After exiting the bus,

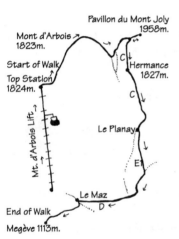

walk up to the lift station and purchase a one-way ticket to Mont d'Arbois, asking for a senior discount if applicable. Take the gondola to the top station at 5985 ft. (1824 m.), where you will find a three-star hotel, restaurants, snack shops and a souvenir store, along with facilities. The view here is unobstructed in all directions, and you can look down the back side of Mont d'Arbois towards le Bettex and le Fayet.

Start: From the top station, turn right in the direction of the sign "Mont Joux - 35 min." The path descends and starts to rise again, and this part of the trail will probably take *Easy Walkers* about 45 minutes. The path is wide, easy to follow, and marked "B." Ski lifts (*télésièges*) can be seen in all directions—Megève is a popular ski resort in winter. The trail continues up to Mont Joux after passing the Chez la Tante restaurant on the right, where additional facilities are available. Do **not** take path A1 down to le Planellet, but continue in the direction of Mont Joly until you come to a path on your right marked "C - Hermance." The path ahead continues up to Mont Joly, and *Easy Walkers* might wish to walk ahead to the Pavillon du Mont Joly for a terrific view and additional facilities.

When ready, return back to the Hermance-C trail, signed "le Planay - Megève par Hermance." It descends down the mountain from 6398 ft. (1950 m.) to 4593 ft. (1400 m.), through Hermance at 5994 ft. (1827 m.). If you look up towards Mont Joly, you will see the famous "snow-duck" above you on the mountain. Local custom dictates that if the neck of the duck is broken (i.e., the snow has melted) by August 15th, the grain farmers will have a good harvest. As you proceed, the trail changes from a wide, dirt path to a narrow, rocky, mountain trail and then reverts back again to a more comfortable path as it descends more rapidly toward le Planay.

> ☞ **HINT: As you descend, make sure your hiking boot laces are tight, and give your knees a rest when needed.**

Make a right turn at the end of the trail on the path towards le Planay. After a few minutes of walking, you will find a nice picnic spot on the left, in a pine forest. When ready, turn left over a little stream on path E1. This path ascends slightly, passing a flower-bedecked farmhouse on your right, as you enter a pretty, pine-needle covered forest path. This part of the trail is level and cool and meets E, where you take a right turn down the hill on a trail with colorful wildflowers on both sides

Eventually you will walk through the meadow on a crushed rock path and reach the road marked D on your map. Turn right on D, walking along the left side of the road, passing through wide, grassy meadows on each side, with

Mont Joly at your back. After about 20 minutes you will reach another road. Turn left and, in the little hamlet of le Maz, opposite the old church with the pretty clock, turn right. This is path D on the map, but it's not marked at the trail, however a sign points to Megève, and it goes directly into the main shopping street. The walk from le Maz to Megève is particularly pretty and takes about 30 minutes, first through the farms and then through the forest.

Walk #4: Lift to Le Jaillet, Walk to Col de Jaillet to Le Christomet to Megève

Walking Easy Time
4 hours

This more challenging walk has a considerable amount of uphill walking, taking *Easy Walkers* from 5200 ft. (1585 m.) to 5774 ft. (1760 m.), with additional ascents and descents until you reach le Christomet at 6070 ft. (1850 m.). The panoramic views from Christomet are worth the extra effort on this ascending trail. You will return to Megève on a descending path, largely through the forest. This is a full day's excursion with picnic and scenery-viewing, but there are **no** facilities between le Jaillet lift station and Megève. Make sure you've packed a picnic lunch and water and taken your map—the hiking trails around Megève correspond to the route letters on the map. If possible, this walk should be taken after a dry period, as the walk down from Christomet through the forest can be wet and slippery.

☞ **HINT:** There is always a point on this trail where you can turn back if you feel the path is too difficult. And remember, the views in the opposite direction are different and just as enthralling!

Directions: Walk past the bus station, turning left up the street past the sports center, then turning right at the last street, marked "Télécabine du Jaillet - piétons." Purchase a one-way ticket, asking for the senior discount if applicable, for the seven-minute ride to the top station in the six-person gondola, which leaves every 30 minutes on the half-hour.

Start: After exiting the gondola, follow the sign for the P route to Col de Jaillet. You will pass a path to the right, R3, the site of another *Easy Walker* hike, but today you will continue walking uphill on P.

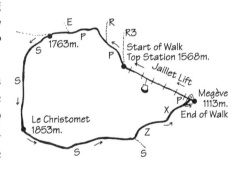

This is a popular, wide, jeep road, and ascends about 655 ft. (200 m.) before leveling off just below Col de Jaillet, where the path meets S to the left to le Christomet. There are many offshooting trails—resist them all—stay on the main path to the intersection with S, to Christomet. You will have walked through open meadows with a profusion of wildflowers and through tall, cool, pine forests, with some great views of Croisse Baulet at 7336 ft. (2236 m.). After making the left turn on path S in the direction of le Christomet, the trail ascends and descends and then rises more steeply to the Christomet peak at 6080 ft. (1853 m.). There are sensational views in all directions—enjoy the panorama.

When ready, continue to your left on S, descending through the forest into Megève. This trail can be steep at times, and it is generally wet in the forest—take your time. Please return to Megève this way only if it has been dry recently—if not, you can return to the lift station at le Jaillet in the same manner in which you came and return to Megève by gondola.

If it is still early, you feel fit, and you haven't taken Walk #1, you can return to Megève (in about $2\frac{1}{2}$ hours) via the directions in Walk #1. Turn left just before the lift station on R3. Turn right past la Ravine restaurant to descend on R2, making a return to Megève on path R at la Fouetta. (See Walk #1 for the full details of this alternate return route.)

Walk #5: Lift to Mont d'Arbois, Walk to Le Bettex Lift, Lift Down to Le Bettex, Walk to Plan Set to Les Berthelets to Pont d'Arbon to Megève

Walking Easy Time
3 hours

While today's *Walking Easy* time is three hours, you should allow at least five to six hours total. This will allow for lunch, two gondola rides, bus transportation, resting and scenery-viewing. You will leave by *navette* (mini-bus) to the Mont d'Arbois lift station and, at the top, take a short walk to another lift for a gondola descent to le Bettex, where the walk begins. Most of the walk descends gently through the forest and meadows overlooking le Fayet and Combloux. Walkers should have a map for this trek, as there are some unmarked entrances to trails and roads. There is a small section of paved-road-walking before returning to Megève by way of Pont d'Arbon—however the road is quiet and rarely used. Pack a picnic lunch and water, of course, as there are no restaurants or facilities between the Bettex lift station and the few hotels along the road to Megève.

Directions: Take the 10:15 am *navette* to Mont d'Arbois from the main bus station next to the Hotel Grange d'Arly. (The long, uphill walk to the lift station is **not** advised.) The gondola operates every 30 minutes on the hour and half-hour—take it to the top station.

Start: Exit the gondola at Mont d'Arbois at 5985 ft. (1824 m.), and walk in the direction of Mont Joux for the short descent and ascent to le Bettex gondola entrance. Up ahead on the left you will see a chairlift that operates only in winter, and the Bettex gondola is adjacent to it. The sign from the road indicating l'Igloo is the starting point for the lift down to le Bettex and, if one wished, con-tinuing all the way to St. Gervais. This lift serves skiers and walkers from the St. Gervais/le Fayet area, trans-porting them up the far side of Mont d'Arbois. It oper-ates every half-hour, at 15 minutes after and 15 minutes before the hour.

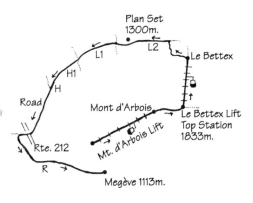

Buy a one-way ticket for the ten-minute gondola ride down to the first stop at le Bettex. For those who wish to extend today's excursion, you can take the cable car down from le Bettex station at 4758 ft. (1450 m.) for a visit to the town of St. Gervais, returning to le Bettex to begin the walk.

At le Bettex, walk down the auto road, past a few shops. You will soon see a red arrow on the left side of the road, on a path. Turn left and follow the red arrow onto a small wagon path. After a few minutes, note a small ski lift and a red arrow pointing down the hill. Turn right and follow the trail down between a few houses to find the trail to the left marked "L2," next to the auto road on your right. Turn left on L2. This delightful walk is well-marked, and is on a fairly level path, traversing cool forests and open, flower-filled meadows at about 4101 ft. (1250 m.).

Continue on L2 until you reach a four-way intersection marked "L" and "L1." Continue on L1 through the forest, soon meeting another four-way intersection where you will turn left on H1. This path remains in the pine forest and descends gently to H, with some pretty views overlooking the valley. The path spills into a small **unmarked** auto road, marked "L" **only** on your map. Turn left on the road, Route du Petit Bois, which soon changes to les Poëx, walking past the Hotel Princesse de Megève on the left (facilities available). Continue to follow this road, winding down and around to the right.

Once you cross over major auto road N212 leading into Megève, you are now walking up on Chemin d'Arbon, passing the Chalet de Vernay on the right. Cross the next, smaller auto road and continue straight ahead past an "R" painted on the old building on your left, passing a chalet and garden, also on the left.

Turn left on a wagon path at a small, orange water pump. This path is signed "Chemin d'Allard." Walk through the meadow, turning left at the first auto road, and go past the summer sledge and le Jaillet lift station. Cross the road leading to Albertville and walk down to the sports center, where you turn right to the bus station.

Walk #6A - Le Leutaz to Chevan to Le Leutaz

Walking Easy Time
3 hours

Walk #6B - Le Leutaz to Chevan to Refuge du Petit Tétraz (Crêt du Midi) to Le Leutaz

Walking Easy Time
5 hours

Walk #6C - Le Leutaz to Chevan to Praz sur Arly

Walking Easy Time
3½ to 5 hours

Today's walk begins at le Leutaz, a little less than three miles (4½ km) from central Megève. Unfortunately, there is no bus service to le Leutaz, and it will be necessary to use a car today, but there are parking facilities at the start of the walk. However, a taxi can also be hired.

Options A and B bring you back to le Leutaz, and if there is no transportation available back to Megève it will be a descending, three-mile walk to the village center on the road. We do not recommend walking up to le Leutaz, but the walk back to Megève is downhill and pleasant. Option C brings you into Praz sur Arly where you can take the bus back to Megève.

The walk from le Leutaz to all options is uphill and will take you from 4429 ft. (1350 m.) to 5414 ft. (1650 m.) at Chevan. However, the degree of ascent is gentle. For those heartier *Easy Walkers*, the trail continues uphill to 5873 ft. (1790 m.) to a *refuge* with a fabulous view, just below Crêt du Midi. Walkers who take option A or B will return to le Leutaz along the same path, this time with impressive views in the opposite direction, including the snow-covered peak of Mont Blanc peeking over the rolling green hills and tall pine forests around Megève.

Directions: After packing a picnic lunch and water (although restaurants and facilities are available along the way), drive from Megève, following the signs to Rochebrune Lift and le Leutaz, both in the same direction. Le Leutaz is about two and one-half miles (4 km) past the lift station. Park on the right side of the road opposite le Chaudron restaurant in le Leutaz.

Start: Walk ahead on the car road, which soon turns into a wide, dirt jeep road, but is also used by those few people who drive up the moun-

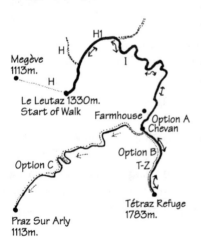

Megève
1113m.

H

Le Leutaz 1330m.
Start of Walk

Farmhouse Option A
Chevan

Option B
T-Z

Option C

Tétraz Refuge
1783m.

Praz Sur Arly
1113m.

tain. This path is lettered "H," but changes to H1 when the H path climbs up the mountain to the left. Continue on H1 until you come to a little wooden bridge on the right with a sign marked "I," in the direction of Col de Véry and Crêt du Midi. Turn right and walk over the bridge.

As you ascend on the path there is a nice view into the valley on your right and the mountains surrounding Megève. To your left and to the rear is the Rochebrune massif, which you will see clearly on your descent. At about 4790 ft. (1460 m.), there is a little working farm and restaurant (Alpage les Vetes) on your right, with a sun terrace and facilities. The path continues to rise gently in the open, arriving at a small farmhouse at 5112 ft. (1558 m.), a perfect spot for a picnic. There are tables for walkers to use for picnicking if they purchase drinks here—fresh milk, soda, mineral water, etc.

The walk continues up to Chevan at 5414 ft. (1650 m.), a scenic viewpoint marked on your map. This is a four-way intersection, where *Easy Walkers* can choose their return option. Options A and B bring walkers back to le Leutaz. Option C is for those who do not have a car at le Leutaz and wish to return to Megève by way of the bus and Praz sur Arly.

Option A: At the four-way intersection at Chevan, *Easy Walkers* will return to le Leutaz on the same path, this time with views of the snow-capped peak of Mont Blanc behind the green hills surrounding Megève.

Option B: For more aggressive walkers, the path straight ahead turns to path T2, going past the restaurant visible up ahead, in the direction of the Crêt du Midi at 6201 ft. (1890 m.). *Easy Walkers* can rest at the *refuge* at 5850 ft. (1783 m.) before turning back on the same trail to le Leutaz. This is the extension for stronger walkers.

Option C: At the four-way intersection, another trail turns down the mountain on the right, just a few feet past the intersection, and takes walkers directly to Praz sur Arly, on paths T2 and T1. Walkers will then take the frequent bus from Praz sur Arly back to Megève.

For more experienced *Easy Walkers*, the following walk was suggested by André Seigneur, the helpful and knowledgeable director of the Megève Tourist Office. Due to time constraints, the authors did not have the opportunity to take this walk.

Walk #7: Le Leutaz to Chevan to Col du Véry to Pré Rosset to L'Alpette to Rochebrune Lift

 Allow a full day for this more demanding walk.

Walkers will need transportation to le Leutaz—available taxis can take you to this starting point. The start of this walk is similar to Walk #6, taking you from le Leutaz on H and H1 to the turnoff, making a right turn on path I, over the little stream, and ascending to the viewpoint at Chevan.

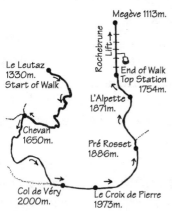

Then, however, you make a sharp left turn at the four-way intersection on T4 to Col de Véry. Take path F along the ridge, staying left at la croix de Pierre at 6473 ft. (1973 m.) and continuing on F to Pré Rosset at 6188 ft. (1886 m.). Take G to l'Alpette at 6139 ft. (1871 m.) and walk down the hill on G to Rochebrune lift station at 5755 ft. (1754 m.) for the ride down to Megève. This is a full day's outing and an early start is necessary. Confirm the closing time of the Rochebrune lift before starting today's hike.

BOURG-SAINT-MAURICE/LES ARCS

The Upper Tarentaise region of the Savoie Alps is the setting for the charming village of Bourg-Saint-Maurice, at 2658 ft.(810 m.), and its mountain neighbors of les Arcs 1600, 1800 and 2000. Situated at the crossroads of some of the world's best winter skiing and summer hiking, Bourg-Saint-Maurice/les Arcs are easily accessible by car and train and offer *Easy Walkers* the entire gamut of summer sports activities and, most importantly, a variety of well-maintained trails for day-hiking.

The traditions of old Savoie are still in evidence in the Bourg-Saint-Maurice area. Baroque churches with ancient frescoes and local museums with old costumes and artifacts are evidence of a rich inheritance.

Each summer Saturday morning, farmers, bakers, and cheese and sausage makers from the surrounding country-side set up a traditional country market in Bourg-Saint-Maurice. You can walk through streets and alleys crowded with local vendors presenting the foods and wines of the re-gion—baskets of freshly picked, prime-quality peaches, to-matoes, lettuce, and melons; wheels of Savoyard cheeses in all shapes, sizes and smells; loaves of country breads; local fresh fish packed in ice; honey from combs to cakes; and dozens of varieties of local sausage (*saucisson*). To this en-ticing mixture of sights and aromas, add the usual prolifera-tion of T-shirt, shoe and apparel stands.

A typical village in the heart of the French Savoie Alps, Bourg-Saint-Maurice can provide *Easy Walkers* with a stimulating outdoor walking holiday. You will discover the natural as well as the cultural resources and treasures of strategically located Bourg-Saint-Maurice—a country village with all the necessary resort amenities, but in an area where herds of cattle are still led to graze each summer in high, alpine pastures.

High above Bourg-Saint-Maurice is a modern invention called les Arcs, linked by an "umbilical cord"—a funicular providing quick, comfortable transportation between the two areas. While Bourg-Saint-Maurice provides the traditional and commercial impetus for the region, les Arcs brings thousands of visitors to the region for summer and winter sporting activities. The French have developed marvelous summer recreation programs at their winter resorts. Sports fields abound, tennis courts are well-used, and children from the ages of one and up are out on the mountain trails, on the trampolines, running in the meadows—all participating in rigourous outdoor sports. There don't seem to be many "couch potatoes" in the French Alps surrounding Bourg-Saint-Maurice/les Arcs!

Les Arcs was the scene of a major downhill ski event in the 1992 Winter Albertville Olympics, with proud evidences everywhere of that honor. The mountain includes three distinct areas, each designated by its altitude—les Arcs 1600 (meters), les Arcs 1800 and les Arcs 2000. The first hotel in Arc 1600 opened in 1968, followed by rapid hotel and apartment development at Arc 1800 and Arc 2000. Arc 1800 is the largest complex within les Arcs, with three sections, Charvet, Villard and Charmettoger. Access to Arc 1600 by an ultra-modern funicular was introduced in 1989, and a free bus system shuttles visitors back and forth between the funicular and the high-altitude Arc villages.

Vacationers can leave Paris in the morning by express train to Bourg-Saint-Maurice, take a bus or funicular to Arc 1600, the shuttle bus to the Arc of their choice, and be in their hotel room in time for dinner—without the hassle of driving! The transportation system and a reasonably priced, all-inclusive discount card (offering holders unlimited use of all operating lifts and the funicular) allow *Easy Walkers* their choice of staying in the more traditional village of Bourg-Saint-Maurice or up on the mountain in les Arcs. There are several three-star hotels in les Arcs and one three-star hotel in a quiet area just outside of Bourg-Saint-Maurice.

Les Arcs is a walker's paradise, some lifts operating every day, others operating three to five days a week. *Easy Walkers* will have the opportunity of rising to 10,499 ft.(3200 m.) at the Aiguille Rouge, with impressive views of the snow-covered Mont Blanc range to the north. Walks can begin and end at the same Arc station or at other Arc stations, but there is always a bus to take you back to your desired location.

You will also have the opportunity of taking an excursion to the internationally famous ski resorts of Tignes and Val d'Isère. Other day excursions from Bourg-Saint-Maurice/les Arcs are available by bus, or by driving to Courmayeur (Italy), to Chamonix through the Mont Blanc Tunnel, to the medieval city of Conflans above Albertville, or to the "Venice of the Savoy Alps," the lovely lake town of Annecy.

Bourg-Saint-Maurice/les Arcs is an outstanding *Easy Walker* base area, and although few Americans have discovered this summer alpine treasure, put a copy of *Walking Easy in the French Alps* in your backpack, brush up on your high school French, and *marche facile.*

Transportation to Bourg-Saint-Maurice/Les Arcs

By Plane: The international airport in Geneva, Switzerland, is 93 miles (150 km) to the north, with car rentals available at the airport. From Geneva Airport to Bourg-Saint-Maurice/les Arcs, pick up superhighway A40 south of Geneva, continuing east until Sallanches where you follow signs to Albertville. Take N212 past Megève to Albertville and drive on N90 east, past Moûtiers, following signs to Bourg-Saint-Maurice. If your hotel is in les Arcs, drive past the Bourg-Saint-Maurice railroad station and follow signs to les Arcs. Once on the mountain, signs will direct you to Arc 1600, Arc 1800 or Arc 2000.

By Car: Bourg-Saint-Maurice/les Arcs is easily accessible by car. The N90 road leads into Bourg through Moûtiers from Albertville, with easy access from all parts of the French Alps and Geneva. Northwestern Italy is traversed through the Aosta Valley and the road over the Col du Petit St. Bernard. While there is train and bus service in this area, you will probably want the convenience of a car, especially if you are staying in Bourg-Saint-Maurice and not in les Arcs.

By Train: From the Paris-Gare-de-Lyon station, a combination of high-speed (TGV) train and local train (change in Chambéry) can bring you to Bourg-Saint-Maurice/les Arcs from Paris in about five hours.

Sample Train Timetable

Dep. Paris	10:47 am
Arr. Chambéry	1:42 pm
Dep. Chambéry	1:55 pm
Arr. Bourg	3:57 pm

Local Bus Service: There is regular bus service from the railroad station at Bourg-Saint-Maurice to Arc 1600, Arc 1800 (Charvet) and Arc 1800 (Villards).

Sample Bus Timetable

Dep. Bourg-St-Maurice	8:30am
Arr. Arc 1600	(on demand)
Arr. Arc 1800 Charvet	9:10 am
Arr. Arc 1800 Villards	9:15 pm

A free shuttle bus (*navette*) runs on a regular schedule from the funicular station at Arc 1600 to Arc 1800 and Arc 2000 and return. Many of these buses are timed to meet the funicular, so a schedule, available at the Tourist Office, is essential.

Activities in Bourg-Saint-Maurice/Les Arcs

This section lists activities available in Bourg-Saint-Maurice and les Arcs on days when additions or alternatives to walking are desired. The Bourg-Saint-Maurice Office du Tourisme is across the street from the railroad station on Place de la Gare, tel: 79-07-04-92. There are also Tourist Offices in Arc 1600 at la Coupole, Arc 2000 in the Galerie Aiguille Rouge, and two in Arc 1800, one in Charvet and one in Villards. These busy Tourist Offices, headed by Jean Marc Silva, can advise *Easy Walkers* about area activities—from local bus schedules to concerts to walking maps.

In Les Arcs: Club des Sports des Arc, with offices in Arc 1600, 1800 and 2000, offers over 30 sporting and cultural activities, for one price. The Carte Verte gives you access to 26 activities from swimming and mountain biking to yoga—and free access to all lifts (*remontées mécaniques*). The Carte Top Tonus offers all the activities in the Carte Verte plus rafting, kayaking, tennis and golf 2000—and free lift access. The Carte Détente offers 19 activites including free lift passes. Check with the Tourist Office in Bourg-Saint-Maurice or the Club des Sports offices in les Arcs for card costs.

In Bourg-Saint-Maurice:

Horseback Riding - Horseback riding is available at le Ranch el Colorado, tel: 79-07-06-05 and at the Centre

Equestre Savournin on route des Arcs/Séez, tel: 79-41-03-09. If you are interested, these centers arrange riding trips into the mountains of the Haute Tarentaise and the Parc National de la Vanoise, with overnight stays at *gîtes* and *refuges*.

Hydro-Electric Plant - You can visit the Centrale Hydro-Electique de Malgovert in Séez, less than two miles from Bourg-Saint-Maurice, with audio-visual exhibits on power in the Haute-Tarentaise Valley. It is open from 9:00 am to noon and 2:00 pm to 5:00 pm, Monday to Friday; 9:00 am to noon on Saturday.

Mini-Golf - It is located near Bourg's outdoor swimming pool and is open from 2:00 pm to 11:00 pm.

Museums - The **Musée du Costume** in Hauteville-Gondon, about one mile from Bourg, is open every day except Tuesday from 2:00 pm to 6:00 pm. The museum features ancient, regional costumes of the Haute Tarentaise area. **Minéraux-Faune de l'Alpe** at 82, avenue Maréchal-Leclerc, Bourg-Saint-Maurice, highlights 20 years of discoveries by Joseph Canova, *cristallier*. It is open every day from 10:00 am to noon and 3:00 pm to 5:00 pm, except Sunday and Monday mornings. **La Maison des Artisans de Séez** is located two miles from Bourg at Place de l'église in the village of Séez, and the hours are 9:00 am to noon and 2:30 pm to 7:00 pm, Monday to Saturday. The museum displays the work of local Savoy artisans.

Swimming - Hours for swimming in Bourg's outdoor pool are Monday to Friday from 10:00 am to 7:30 pm, Saturday and Sunday from noon to 7:30 pm.

Tennis - Call the Tennis Club de Bourg-Saint-Maurice at 79-07-31-45 for information and reservations.

Excursions in and around Bourg-Saint-Maurice/Les Arcs

This section introduces day excursions for *Easy Walkers* to enjoy when the weather is not suitable for high-altitude walking, or if an alternative to walking is desired. Be sure to check current timetables for best connections if using local transportation.

1. Lifts in Bourg-Saint-Maurice/Les Arcs

A) From Bourg-Saint-Maurice: The **Funiculaire Bourg-St-Maurice** rises from Bourg at 2658 ft. (810 m.) to Arc 1600 at 5250 ft. (1600 m.). It operates every day from 8:30 am to 7:30 pm, and leaves in both directions every half-hour on the hour.

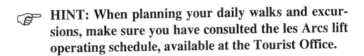 HINT: When planning your daily walks and excursions, make sure you have consulted the les Arcs lift operating schedule, available at the Tourist Office.

B) From Arc 1600: The continuously moving chairlift, **Télésiège Débrayable de la Cachette**, accesses the Arpette plateau and rises from 5292 ft. (1613 m.) to 7087 ft. (2160 m.), running every day in summer from 9:15 am to 12:30 pm and 1:30 pm to 5:00 pm. The **Télésiège des Combettes** chairlift rises from 5309 ft. (1618 m.) to 5778 ft. (1760 m.) and is open in summer Sunday to Thursday from 10:00 am to noon and 2:00 pm to 6:00 pm, Saturday 2:00 pm to 6:00 pm.

C) From Arc 1800: The **Télécabine Transarc** gondola runs every day in summer from 9:15 am to 12:30 pm and 1:30 pm to 4:45 pm. It rises from 5617 ft. (1712 m.) to 8367 ft.(2550 m.) with an intermediate stop.

D) From Arc 2000: The **Télésiège Dou de l'Homme** chairlift is open Tuesday, Thursday and Sunday from 9:30 am to 4:45 pm during July and August. Moving continuously, it rises from 7087 ft. (2180 m.) to 8744 ft. (2665 m.) and the mid-station for access to the Aiguille Rouge. The **Télésiège Debrayable des Plagnettes** operates on Monday, Wednesday, Friday and Saturday. This chairlift rises from 7153 ft. (2180 m.) to 8367 ft. (2550 m.), near the top station of the Transarc gondola lift. The **Téléphérique de l'Aiguille Rouge** cable car operates Tuesday, Thursday and Sunday in summer, from 9:45 am to 4:30 pm, rising from 8760 ft. (2670 m.) to 10,585 ft. (3226 m.). You should allow about two hours for the ascent, descent and viewing at the Aiguille Rouge, and weather conditions should be clear and dry for this trip. It is not usually cold at the top, but sunscreen and sunglasses are a must.

☞ **HINT: A seven-day pass allowing unlimited access to the funicular and ALL lifts costs 390 FF (in 1994)—a good buy for *Easy Walkers*, especially if your hotel is down in Bourg-Saint-Maurice and you take the funicular up and back for walks in the les Arcs area.**

2. Tignes - Tignes is a thoroughly modern village. Its oldest buildings were built only 45 years ago, with the construction of a large hydroelectric dam, when the old village of Tignes was destroyed and rebuilt 1000 feet (305 m.) higher, next to a small lake. The largest fresco in the world is painted on the wall of the dam—representing the strength of the ancient world and the energy of the modern world. Tignes offers summer skiing, lake water sports and the highest 18-hole golf course in Europe. (See Walk #6 for more details.)

Directions: By car - Take N90 northeast out of Bourg-Saint-Maurice, following signs on D902 southeast 15 miles (24 km) into Tignes. By bus - The 8:30 am bus from Bourg arrives in Tignes-le-Lac at 9:15 am. To return, there is a 2:45 pm bus arriving at 3:40 pm and a 6:30 pm bus arriving in Bourg at 7:50 pm.

3. Val d'Isère - Although skiing plays a central role in Val d'Isère's winter life, summer brings hikers and sightseers to this mountain village. Ascend on the cable car to Rocher de Bellevarde for outstanding views of the upper Tarentaise region and the Vanoise National Park. (See Walk #6 for more details.) On the way to Val-d'Isère, stop to view the hydroelectric dam at Tignes—with the largest fresco in the world painted on its wall.

    Directions: By car - Take N90 through Séez to D902 southeast, past Tignes, for the 25-mile (40-km) drive to Val d'Isère. By bus - The 8:30 am bus arrives in Val d'Isère at 9:40 am. To return, the 3:00 pm bus arrives in Bourg at 3:50 pm.

4. Annecy - See the "Chamonix" chapter, Excursion #4.

    Directions: By car - Follow N90 through Moûtiers into Albertville. Outside of Albertville, pick up N212 north to N508, taking you around the lake to Annecy. To return, drive around the other side of the lake on D909 before picking up N508, then reverse the above directions to return to Albertville and Bourg/les Arcs.

5. Courchevel - See the "Méribel" chapter, Excursion #6.

    Directions: By car - Take N90 out of Bourg towards Moûtiers. Follow signs to Courchevel and drive south on the winding, local road to the Courchevels.

6. Albertville - See the "Megève" chapter, Excursion #5.

    Directions: By car - Take N90 west into Albertville, where you may follow signs to the medieval city of Conflans and/or the Olympic site. By train - The 8:26 am train from Bourg arrives in Albertville at 9:29 am, the next train at 10:48 am arrives at 11:53 am. To return, there is a 4:37 pm train arriving in Bourg at 5:55 pm.

7. Belleville Valley Towns - The Vallée de Belleville is composed of 24 small alpine villages and two mega-ski resorts—**Val Thorens** and **les Menuires**. Val Thorens at 7546 ft. (2300 m.), is the highest altitude resort in Western Europe, and its summer scenery, without the dazzling snow-cover of winter, can be stark and harsh because it lies above the tree-line. The **Val-Thorens Téléphérique de Caron** rises to 10,499 ft. (3200 m.), while in les Menuires at 5955 ft. (1815 m.), the **Télécabine de la Masse, des Bruyères et du Mont de la Chambre** rises to 9351 ft. (2850 m.). **St. Martin de Belleville** is an authentic Savoie village nestled in the center of the valley, whose residents preserve the history and heritage of the past with festivals and fairs. Visit the ancient church in St. Martin de Belleville and the Church of Notre Dame on the way to les Menuires.

Directions: By car - Take N90 west, following signs in Moûtiers to Vallée de Belleville, picking up local road D915 south through St. Martin-de-Belleville, les Menuires, and finally, Val-Thorens.

8. Chamonix - This world capital of mountaineering is dominated by the powerful majesty of Mont Blanc, the highest mountain in Europe—but the town successfully combines boutiques, restaurants, hotels and services of a large resort with the incomparable, awesome, natural surroundings of the Mont Blanc massif, the highest mountain in Europe. (See the "Chamonix" chapter for more details.)

Directions: By car - Take N90 northeast over the Italian border, following signs to Courmayeur, Italy, and the Mont Blanc Tunnel. Drive through the tunnel, which brings you outside of Chamonix.

☞ **HINT: Remember your passport if you are leaving France on this or any other excursion!**

9. Courmayeur, Italy - Only 37 miles (60 km) northeast of Bourg/les Arcs, Courmayeur is a well-known summer and winter resort at the foot of Mont Blanc. (For more details, see "Chamonix," Excursion #7.)

    Directions: By car - Follow D90 northeast, going over the Italian border and Col du Petit St. Bernard, then pick up S26 into Courmayeur. By bus - Take the 8:30 am bus from Bourg, arriving in Courmayeur at 10:10 am. To return, there is a 4:00 pm bus, arriving in Bourg at 6:45 pm.

10. Col du Petit St-Bernard - The **Jardin de la Chanousia** is at 7120 ft. (2170 m.), only 18 miles (30 km) east of the Col. The garden was started in 1897 by the abbot Pierre Chanoux, abandoned in 1940, but redeveloped in 1976, and contains over 1200 species of alpine plants and flowers. It is open in July and August only.

    Directions: By car - Take N90 east over the winding road past la Rosière at 6070 ft. (1850 m.) to the Col, just over the Italian border.

11. Peisey-Nancroix - Visit **la Chapelle des Vernettes**, dating from 1722 and built at an altitude of 5906 ft. (1800 m.). Note its beautiful cupola and magnificent old poly-chrome, recently restored.

    Directions: By car - Take N90 southwest out of Bourg, following directions on the winding local road to Peisey.

12. Hauteville-Gondon - The Baroque **Eglise d'Hauteville-Gondon** dates from 1694, while the **Eglise de Peisey** was built even earlier, in 1685. Visit the **costume museum** for exhibits of how people dressed in years gone by in the Haute-Tarentaise area.

    Directions: By car - Take the narrow, winding local road south into Hauteville.

13. Gran Paradiso National Park, Italy - See "Chamonix," Excursion #8.

Directions: By car - Take N90 east over the Italian border, which becomes S26 in Italy. Turn east on S26 towards Aosta, into the Aosta Valley. Make a right turn at Aymavilles, about four miles (6 km) west of Aosta, climbing into the Val di Cogne. Twelve miles (20 km) up into the valley is the village of Cogne at 5033 ft. (1534 m.), a good place to stop and enjoy the beauty and solitude of the park.

14. Aosta, Italy - See "Chamonix," Excursion #9.

Directions: By car - Take N90 east over the Italian border, becoming S26 in Italy. Turn east on S26 into Aosta. By bus - There is an 8:30 am bus arriving in Aosta at 11:15 am. To return, the bus leaves at 4:00 pm and is in Bourg at 7:30 pm.

15. Chambéry - The capital of the Duchy of Savoy from the 13th to the 17th centuries, Chambéry is an appealing, small city of handsome arcades, squares and shopping streets. Its famous **Elephant Fountain (Fontaine des Éléphants)** is situated in the center of town and it commemorates a trip to India made by a local hero. At the other end of the Boulevard de la Colonne from the Elephant Fountain is the Tourist Office. **Château des Ducs de Savoie**, built in the 14th century, in the southwest corner of the old town, was the residence of the former dukes, and it towers over the city. Guided tours to the Château are mandatory—check with the Tourist Office for information. However, *Easy Walkers* might enjoy climbing the 200 steps of **Round Tower** for a terrific view of the city.

Directions: By car - Follow N90 through Moûtiers and Albertville. In Albertville take A430 south, leading to A43 into Chambéry. By train - The 8:26 am train arrives in Chambéry at 10:16 am, and a 4:06 pm train returns to Bourg at 5:55 pm.

16. Aix-les-Bains - Only ten miles (16 km) north of Chambéry, one of France's largest and most fashionable spa-towns is set on the eastern shores of Lac du Bourget, at the foot of the Alps. The Tourist Office (Syndicat d'Initiative) on place Maurice-Mollard, can provide you with information about the hot-water springs which are said to help arthritis. This is a pretty town, with colorful gardens, casinos, a race course and a golf course, as well as a beach for swimming on the lake.

If there is time, you can take a four-hour boat ride on the lake, including a visit to the **Abbaye de Hautecombe** in Chindrieux, the mausoleum of many of the nobility of the House of Savoy, built on a cliff jutting into the lake. Check with the Tourist Office for boat schedules. **Musée Faure**, on bd. des Côtes, boasts an interesting collection of modern art, including Rodin sculptures. It is open every day but Tuesday, 9:30 am to noon and 2:00 pm to 6:00 pm, with an admission charge.

Directions: By car - Follow N90 through Albertville, then A430 to A43 past Chambéry, taking the local road into Aix. By train - Take the 8:26 am train to Chambéry, arriving at 10:16 am, and change for the 10:30 am train to Aix, arriving at 10:40 am. To return, if you take the 3:53 pm train, it arrives in Bourg without a change at 5:55 pm.

17. Great Saint Bernard Pass and Hospice, Switzerland - See "Chamonix," Excursion #11.

Directions: By car - Follow N90 northeast over the Col du Petit St-Bernard and the Italian border, where the road changes to S26. Continue north until the road splits and take S26 into Aosta. Drive north on S27 but do not drive through the St. Bernard Tunnel—take the old, winding road to the Hospice, right over the Swiss border.

18. Bus Excursions - Transports Martin, located in the railroad station, tel: 79-07-04-49, runs bus excursions from Bourg-Saint-Maurice to the following places: Aix-les-Bains and Abbaye de Hautecombe; Annecy and Musée du

Château; Chamonix, Tunnel du Mont Blanc and Courmayeur; Lac de Tignes; Val d'Isère; Col de l'Iseran and Bonneval-sur-Arc; la Rosière; Hauteville and the Musée du Costume Savoyard; Albertville, Conflans and Beaufort; Aosta; Tour du Parc National de la Vanoise and Tour du Mont Blanc.

Bourg-Saint-Maurice/Les Arcs Walks

Recommended Maps:
1) Sentiers de Moyenne Montagne en Haute-Tarentaise
2) Cartes des Promenades à Pied - à V.T.T - Les Arcs, Bourg Saint Maurice, Savoie, France, Peisey-Vallandry
3) IGN #3532 - Les Arcs, La Plagne

The first two maps listed above are available at the local Tourist Offices and give directions for promenades (easy walks, many on paved roads) and *randonnées* (generally away from paved roads on meadow and mountain paths). The IGN map is available in newpaper and book stores and is a precise hiking map of the area. If your base village is Bourg-Saint-Maurice, you might wish to have all three maps. If your base village is les Arcs, the last two should be sufficient.

☞ **HINT: Walking in the Bourg-Saint-Maurice/les Arcs area requires a transportation strategy. Many walks begin and end at the different les Arcs stations where you can take advantage of the fabulous, free bus system between Arc 1600, Arc 1800 and Arc 2000. If you are staying in Bourg-Saint-Maurice, you will travel up to Arc 1600 by the funicular in back of the train station, and take the free *navette* to any one of the Arc stations. It is also possible to drive to the Arcs, however the authors found it best to use the available public transportation, leaving your car at your base village—either Bourg-Saint-Maurice or les Arcs.**

Directions to all walks beginning in les Arcs, departing from Bourg-Saint-Maurice by funicular: Follow the

Funiculaire signs on the main auto road in the center of the village, near the railroad station, bringing you to a large parking area. Park your car and follow the sign reading "Funiculaire Access" at the far end of the parking area. A covered passage takes you over the railroad tracks to the funicular station. This modern system leaves Bourg for Arc 1600 (and Arc 1600 for Bourg) every half-hour on the hour, starting at 8:30 am, with the last descent to Bourg at 7:30 pm. After leaving the Arc 1600 funicular station, turn left to catch the bus to either Arc 1800 or Arc 2000. We strongly suggest you pick up a current les Arcs funicular and bus timetable at the Tourist Office.

Walk #1: Top Station Transarc Lift, Walk to Col de la Chal to Lac Marloup to Arc 2000

Walking Easy Time
3 hours
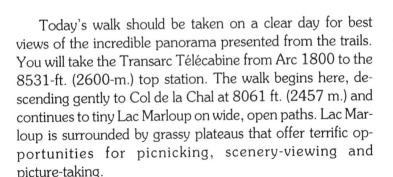

Today's walk should be taken on a clear day for best views of the incredible panorama presented from the trails. You will take the Transarc Télécabine from Arc 1800 to the 8531-ft. (2600-m.) top station. The walk begins here, descending gently to Col de la Chal at 8061 ft. (2457 m.) and continues to tiny Lac Marloup on wide, open paths. Lac Marloup is surrounded by grassy plateaus that offer terrific opportunities for picnicking, scenery-viewing and picture-taking.

After passing Lac Marloup you will see the chairlift rising towards the Aiguille Rouge at 10,588 ft. (3227 m.), surrounded on three sides by glaciers. If you look carefully up on the mountain to your right, you will be able to see the protruding receiving station for the cable car that rises up from the Arc 2000 mid-station to the peak. The walk ends at Arc 2000, as you descend the mountain on a wide, comfortable, popular path. Plan the better part of the day for today's walk, and stow your picnic lunch in your backpack. There is a restaurant with a sun terrace and facilities at the Transarc top station, but nothing else is available until you reach your destination at Arc 2000, where you take the shuttle bus to Arc 1600 and the funicular down to Bourg, or another bus to Arc 1800 and your hotel.

Directions: From Bourg-Saint-Maurice, follow the funicular directions indicated above and take the bus to Arc 1800, getting off at the last stop. If you are staying in les Arcs 1800, drive your car to the parking area closest to the Transarc Lift. Walk up to the Transarc Gondola and, if you haven't purchased a seven-day pass, buy a one-way ticket to the top station. Take the Arc 1800 Transarc Télécabine, staying on the gondola to the top station at 8531 ft. (2600 m.). This location is the start of many walks in the les Arcs region.

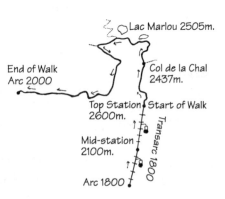

Start: Walk straight ahead, following signs to Col de la Chal and Lac Marloup (sometimes spelled Marlou), and descend to a large, grassy plateau and a wide, dirt path. At a signed intersection, turn left towards Lac Marloup. You will pass two teeny-tiny lakes before reaching Lac Marloup, its blue waters reflecting the mountains and hillsides around it. Photographers will have opportunities to record the mountain panorama, including the imposing Mont Blanc in the distance, and there are many picnic opportunities around the lake.

When ready, continue on the path, and you will soon be able to see the chairlift operating up to the modern cable car station high on your right. A cable car leaves that mid-station, ascending to the Aiguille Rouge at 10,588 ft. (3227 m.), a *Walking Easy* excursion on another day. Continue straight ahead on the path until you arrive at a sharp left turn, down the mountain, around the Plan de l'Homme.

> ☞ **HINT: Make sure you turn left on the wide, descending path—it is unmarked—bringing you to Arc 2000. Do not continue ahead, under the chairlift.**

This path circles down and around another small lake on your right, with the chalets of Arc 2000 in view. Descend to the base station of the chairlift you saw earlier and walk past it into the center of Arc 2000. A walk down the steps at the end of the shops and cafés brings you to the bus stop for Arc 1600 and the funicular down to Bourg, or the bus to Arc 1800 (with a transfer at Arc 1600) and your hotel.

Walk #2: Excursion to Aiguille Rouge, Walk Mid-Station to Lac Marloup to Transarc Top Station, Return to Arc 1800 (Optional Walk Mid-Station to Arc 1800)

   Walking Easy Time
2 to 3 hours

Today's walk is not long and does not require an early start. It does however, require a bright, clear day. You will leave from Arc 2000 on a chairlift to the mid-station at 8695 ft. (2650 m.), transferring to a cable car that ascends to the Aiguille Rouge at 10,588 ft. (3227 m.). A quick climb through a small snowfield to the ridge reveals unparalleled panoramic views of the surrounding glaciers, Mont Pourri in the Vanoise National Park, and the dominating Mont Blanc range to the north.

Easy Walkers will return to the mid-station by cable car to continue today's walk, descending easily on a nicely graded, zig-zagging path under the Aiguille Rouge to the main walking path. The walk finishes with a pass by Lac Marloup at 8203 ft. (2500 m.) and a walk up to the top station of the Transarc gondola to return to Arc 1800.

> ☞ **HINT: Insulated jackets are not needed at the top today—even a sweatshirt can be too warm in the summer—but stow one in your backpack just in case. You do need suntan lotion and sunglasses, however.**

Directions: From Bourg-Saint-Maurice, follow the directions indicated above to Arc 1600 and take the shuttle bus to Arc 2000. For those in Arc 1800, take the free bus to Arc 1600 and change for the bus to Arc 2000.

Start: After leaving the bus at Arc 2000, walk up the steps and through the Arc 2000 sports center. You will probably see all types of sports activities for young people and adults, sponsored by Club des Sport of les Arcs. This organization provides a wide variety of daily activities, employs over 100 counselors, and is widely used by visitors to the area.

Continue past the small shops to a wide dirt path ahead for a 15-minute walk, following signed directions to Dou de l'Homme chairlift. On your left, notice the markings of the 1992 winter Olympics—the torch, the flags, and the downhill ski runs—as you pass under several ski lifts not operating in the summer. Look high to the left and you can see the Aiguille Rouge cable station protruding over the mountain, your destination.

At the chairlift, remove your backpack, stepping on the wooden platform and allowing the chair to sweep under you. Pull down the metal bar above you and put your feet on the footrest. During the comfortable 18-minute ride to the mid-station you can see in the distance to your right the Transarc top station (you will walk here after your excursion to the Aiguille Rouge). Just before arriving at the mid-station, take your feet off the footrest, lift the bar and move quickly out of the way of the passing chair.

Up to your left note the sign for Aiguille Rouge, the station for the cable car to the top. Climb the stairs and enter the cable car, which leaves every 20 minutes for the five-minute ascent to the top station at 10,588 ft. (3227 m.).

After exiting the cable car, walk carefully over the little snow and rock field to the peak. Just below the Aiguille Rouge and down to your left is the Glacier du Varet at 10,171 ft. (3100 m.). To the right and in front of towering 11,086-foot (3379-meter) Mont Pourri are two glaciers, Grand Col and Geay. The area to the right, including Mont Pourri, is in the Vanoise National Park, which becomes Gran Paradiso Park at the Italian border. To the north looms the *grand-père* of them all—the peaks of the Mont Blanc range. Take enough time to absorb the scene around you.

Return to the mid-station by cable car, following the sign reading *sortie*, walking back down the steps you climbed earlier. Turn right on the dirt jeep road and follow the wide, well-graded, zig-zag path down to the main trail, where you turn left and descend gently to the small, clear reflecting lake—Marloup—sitting in the midst of a grassy plateau. Once again, there are great views of Mont Blanc and many picnic opportunities here.

Continue on the path as it descends easily to the Col de la Chal, in the direction of the top station of the Transarc gondola, visible ahead. The wide path then ascends until you reach a restaurant with a sun terrace and facilities and the Transarc lift station. Take the gondola down to the base station at Arc 1800. If you are staying in Bourg, take the convenient les Arcs shuttle bus, just below the lift station, back to Arc 1600 and the funicular down to Bourg-Saint-Maurice.

There is an option to extend this walk. Follow the "Les-Arcs: Walking, Bicycle" map and exit at the mid-station of the Transarc gondola. Walk down to Arc 1800 on path #5 to your left to the intersection, where you turn right. After walking under five lifts, take path #4 down to Arc 1800.

Walk #3: Arc 2000 to Arc 1600

Walking Easy Time
3 hours

Arc 2000 is the starting point for a walk through the forest and along the Chemin du Canal, to Arc 1600. This is a gentle descent of 1312 ft. (400 m.) on a wide path shared with mountain bikers. The path, lined with tall, bright purple flowers in summer, is mostly through the shady forest and is blazed all the way.

Directions: Follow the previously indicated directions to Arc 2000, making sure you have checked the current bus and funicular schedule.

Start: After leaving the bus, walk up the steps and through the sports fields of Arc 2000, noting the Olympic torch and flags on the left and continuing ahead until you see a sign for Pré St. Esprit. Follow the path down to the right, with the tennis courts off to your left. You will walk under non-operating ski lifts and then turn down a narrow, descending, mountain trail towards the rapidly running stream. As you continue to walk, you will be in full view of Mont Blanc to the north.

Turn left at the intersection, walking on a wide dirt path for about 50 meters to the Bois de l'Ours chairlift and a group of signs pointing to Arc 1600 and Pré St. Esprit to your right. This wide path continues all the way to Arc 1600, with few diversions. If you are unsure of a marking, **always** follow the blue bike signs with an Indian headress emblazoned on them.

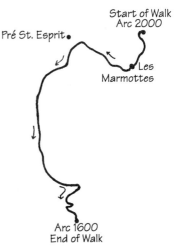

You will pass a little road that takes you down to Pré St. Esprit with its restaurant and sun terrace. If you don't want a snack, remain on the main path, staying out of the way of bikers. The path sometimes meets the road, but continue walking on the main trail, blazed yellow, with blue directional signs for bicyclists.

At an intersection, follow the sign for Arc 1600, bringing you to the Hotel Beguin. Walk on the road to the right, buttonhooking to a lower road to the left, quickly noting the blaze and bicycle sign taking you sharply down on a narrow trail through the forest. This trail shortly ends at another paved road. Follow the yellow blaze and blue sign to the right and enter the forest again on a descending path leading to another road and Arc 1600. Turn left and immediately enter the gravel path to the right, turning right again to the funicular to Bourg-Saint-Maurice, or to the shuttle bus to other les Arcs stations.

Walk #4: Mid-Station Transarc Lift to L'Arpette to Arc 1600

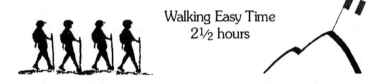

Walking Easy Time
2½ hours

This gentle walk starts from the mid-station of the Arc 1800 Transarc gondola on a wide path beginning at 6890 ft. (2100 m.), descending easily to Arc 1600 along the middle balcony of the mountain and offering continuous views of the Mont Blanc range. There are additional views of Bourg-Saint-Maurice dominating the valley below, as well as the three villages of Arc 1800—Charmettoger, les Villards and Charvet. You also will walk under a half-dozen ski lifts that serve winter sports enthusiasts.

A delightful restaurant with a sun terrace and facilities is along this path, with lovely views of the valley. The walk continues on the Chemin des Sources, past the tennis complex above Arc 1600. Since this is an easy, half-day excursion, you might wish to take the Cachette chairlift at Arc 1600 to the station below le Signal des Têtes at 7054 ft. (2150 m.). This station provides a somewhat higher view over the area you just walked and can be the starting point for a more demanding hike around the peak of le Signal des Têtes, taking the lift down to Arc 1600 for the return.

Directions: From Bourg-Saint-Maurice, take the funicular to Arc 1600. Turn left to the shuttle bus area and take the bus to Arc 1800. Exit the bus at the last stop in Arc 1800, walk up the steps on your right to the Transarc gondola station and disembark at the mid-station, as the gondola moves slowly through the station.

Start: Walk out of the station and to your right, following the walker's sign to Arc 1600. The walk begins with a gentle, 15-minute ascent on a wide path, with views of the Arc 1800 18-hole golf course down on the left. You have continuous views of the Mont Blanc range in front of you as you walk in a northerly direction. You will soon arrive at a modern, terraced, wooden chalet, with the flags of the l'Arpette res-taurant below you

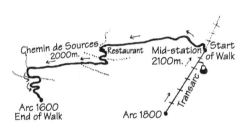

on the left. Follow the road around and down to the left, continuing as it zig-zags back and forth under the Mont Blanc chairlift (closed for the summer).

> ☞ **HINT: Before you descend under the restaurant, you might see a walker's sign that indicates Arc 1600 to the right and Arc 1800 to the left, but *Easy Walkers* will ignore that first sign and take the road turning below the restaurant, walking underneath the Mont Blanc chairlift twice.**

As you proceed, you will be able to see Arc 1800 down to the left and Bourg-Saint-Maurice sitting in the valley be-low. The road forks to Arc 1800 down to the left, but *Easy*

Walkers will continue straight ahead, in the signed direction of Arc 1600. The path is blazed yellow and goes in and out of forested areas and meadows filled with tall, purple flowers, continuing to descend towards Arc 1600. Walk under an operating ski lift, one that you might choose to take later to visit le Signal des Têtes.

At the intersection ahead, turn left toward the tennis courts and right again on the main path, as the path splits left for skiers. Keep the tennis courts on your right as you descend. At another intersection follow the sign for Arc 1600 to the left to the small auto road. Turn right, past the Hotel Beguin, and left again on the lower auto road. Immediately note the yellow blaze and blue bicycle sign with indian headress, pointing down a narrow, forest path (it is only steep for a few seconds).

This trail meets an auto road—follow the yellow blaze to the right and down again into the forest, to an Arc 1600 paved road. Turn left, and immediately right onto the gravel path. If you wish, the Cachette chairlift is straight ahead for an excursion to le Signal des Têtes. Or, turn right to take the funicular to Bourg-Saint-Maurice and the shuttle bus to other les Arcs stations. For those who are staying in les Arcs, this might be a good time to take the funicular down and visit Bourg-Saint-Maurice. Make sure you check the timetables.

Walk #5: Transarc Mid-Station to Bergerie du Rey through Forêt de Plan Peisey to La Maitaz to Arc 1800

Walking Easy Time
2½ to 3½ hours

Depart from Arc 1800 on the Transarc gondola to the mid-station. After getting off the lift, head south, taking the path down in the direction of Bergerie du Rey and Nancroix. After the first descent from the mid-station, take the left fork on trail #5 on the "Carte des Promenades Les Arc-à Pied-à V.T.T." map, walking under a ski lift and passing a restaurant on your right, to the intersection.

There are two options for *Easy Walkers* to return to Arc 1800. You may either buttonhook around to the right and walk left at the fork, on a combined walking and bike path, passing Praz Pellier to la Maitaz and turning right again towards Arc 1800. Or, at the intersection, continue ahead and down into the Forêt de Plan Peisey. Turn right at another intersection by Plan Peisey, walk under four ski lifts to la Maitaz, and straight ahead into Arc 1800.

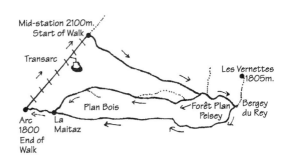

Walk #6: Excursion to Tignes and Val d'Isère

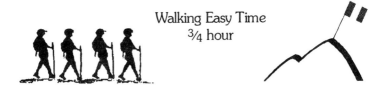

Walking Easy Time
¾ hour

Because the internationally famous ski centers of Val d'Isère and Tignes are so close to Bourg-Saint-Maurice/les Arcs, we think it is interesting to pay them a visit, for walking as well as sightseeing.

Directions: Leave Bourg-Saint-Mauric/les Arcs on N90, the main road, following signs to Tignes and Val d'Isère. Drive through the little village of Séez, and climb on #902 through Saint-Foy, past the reservoir at Tignes, all the way to Val d'Isère at 6037 ft. (1840 m.). Val d'Isère is bordered by peaks of up to 11,155 ft. (3400 m.) and serves as the entrance to a mountain pass close to Italy, the Col de l'Iseran at 9088 ft. (2770 m.). At Val d'Isère you might wish to ascend on the cable car to Rocher de Bellevarde for views of the upper Tarentaise region and the Vanoise National Park. There is also a nice drive between Val d'Isère and Tignes, the auto road ascending from the middle of the road along the large lake, up to Lake Saut at 7546 ft. (2300 m.), with a convenient parking area. There are great views from here, and some gentle walking is available.

Drive back towards Tignes and park at the area overlooking the large dam on your left, for views of this remarkable sight. The largest fresco in the world is painted on the wall of the dam, representing the strength of the ancient world and the energy of the modern one. Continue driving over the dam, following the signs to Tignes-le-Lac at 6890 ft. (2100 m.). Park close to the lake, right before the open mountain tunnel.

Start: Just behind you, on the hill, are signs describing walks in this area, but first you can enjoy a gentle, 45-minute walk on the path around the lake. Returning to the hiking signs, stronger walkers might wish to ascend to Col du Palet at 8705 ft. (2653 m.), a rise of 1837 ft. (560 m.). Going and coming on the same path, providing you reach the Col du Palet, will take about four hours. Return to the main road for the drive to Bourg-Saint-Maurice/les Arcs.

There are many additional hikes for *Easy Walkers* to enjoy in the les Arcs area. If you're interested, be sure to purchase the walking map "Carte des Promenades - Les Arcs."

MÉRIBEL

When Glenn Miller's great orchestra of the 1930s and '40s played "String of Pearls," we doubt they had the Méribel Valley in mind, but perhaps they should have. Thirteen small villages and hamlets are strung throughout this valley, recessed between two imposing mountain ranges. Nestled on the mountainside, Méribel is composed of four districts: Méribel Centre, Altiport, Belvédère, and Méribel-Mottaret, with altitudes from 4593 ft. (1400) at la Chaudanne to 5578 ft. (1700 m.) at Méribel-Mottaret—whose hotels and high-rise condominiums were built beneath the towering Aiguille du Fruit. Méribel's strict zoning code has prescribed traditional alpine design, preserving a unity of style in the resort with charming, Savoyard/chalet architecture, using warmly shaded pine and rough-hewn stone.

Originally a tiny farming community, Méribel's winter sports possibilities were discovered by the British when their customary ski slopes in Austria were invaded by Germany in 1938. The four districts of Méribel are essentially new inventions for these winter sports enthusiasts, with few reminders of centuries gone by. Still, Méribel has a style, warmth and charm that the neighboring ski mega-centers of Courchevel, Val-Thorens and les Menuires forgot to consider in the rush to house their thousands of winter visitors. Méribel also recognizes that there is life after ski season, and provides the frequent and free summer Méribus to transport walkers between its districts, and the Méribel Tourist Office closely supervises the hiking trails, their signs and walking maps.

Méribel is the center of the Trois Vallées (the Three Valleys). The internationally famous ski resort of Courchevel lies in one adjacent valley, Val-Thorens, at 7546 ft. (2300 m.) the highest ski resort in Europe, in the other. The Trois Vallées is reputed to be the largest ski complex in the world, and with a single pass skiers have access to all the ski lifts and runs in the area. The five resorts of the Trois Vallées—Méribel, Courchevel, Val Thorens, les Menuires, la Tania—provide over 370 miles (600 km) of marked ski runs with 200 lifts, including three cable cars, 30 gondolas, and 167 chair- and drag-lifts. A thousand ski instructors work daily in this skiers' paradise—with the capacity to service 220,000 skiers per hour!

Vanoise National Park is bordered on the west by the Méribel Valley and includes a natural reserve with Lake Tuéda and Mont du Vallon at 9686 ft. (2952 m.), where *Easy Walkers* will hike. Walking in the Méribel Valley is not always easy, the trails have many ascents and descents, but most are within the range of *Easy Walkers*.

Transportation to Méribel

By Plane: Geneva Airport is located 85 miles (135 km) to the north of Méribel. It is more convenient to rent a car at the airport and drive to Méribel than to use train or bus connections. From Geneva's Cointrin Airport take super-highway A40 east, picking up N212 south before Sallanches. Follow signs to, and drive past, Megève and Albertville, where you take N90 through Moûtiers to the local road to Méribel. Drive towards Méribel Centre, following signs to Altiport and then le Belvédère, if that is where your hotel is located.

By Train/Bus: Méribel is 12 miles (18 km) from the Moûtiers train station, which services TGV (high-speed) trains to and from Paris. During the summer there are three buses a day to and from the Moûtiers train station to Méribel.

Sample Bus Schedule

Dep. Moûtiers Train Station	7:45 am
Arr. Méribel Centre	8:15 am
Dep. Méribel Centre	9:15 am
Arr. Moûtiers Train Station	9:45 am

By Car: From southern or western France, drive to Albertville, taking N90 southeast to Moûtiers and picking up the local road into Méribel. From the north, take N212 into Albertville, then N90 southeast into Moûtiers, watching for the Méribel signs.

From the Aosta Valley in Italy, drive on S26 and take it south, winding over Col du Petit St. Bernard and the French border, past Bourg St-Maurice. Pick up N90 towards Moûtiers, watching for signs to Méribel.

Méribus (Navette Vallée de Méribel): Shuttle buses run throughout the resort, stopping at the Altiport, Belvédère, Méribel Tourist Office, la Chaudanne area, Bois d'Arbin, Méribel-Mottaret and Mottaret-Hameau. Many of the lifts are also served by these scheduled, free shuttle buses. The red dots on the village map in back of the "Bienvenue à Méribel - Welcome to Méribel" brochure, indicate the bus stops. The Tourist Office will supply a bus schedule, and there is also an operating schedule printed in the brochure.

Sample Méribus Schedule

Altiport	9:20 am
Belvédère	9:25 am
Tourist Office	9:40 am
Méribel-Mottaret	9:50 am

Activities in Méribel

This section lists activities available in Méribel on days when additions or alternatives to walking are desired. The very active and helpful Méribel Tourist Bureau (Office du Tourisme) is located in the center of the resort, tel: 79-08-60-01. A Multi-Activities Card (Carte Multi-Loisirs) can be bought at the Tourist Office. This six-day card includes three games at Crazy Golf, two archery sessions, free access to the swimming pool and ice stadium, a discount on horseback riding at Bois d'Arbin, one forest outing with the forest warden, plus additional discounts on various activities—cost: 420 FF.

Archery - The archery area at Méribel-Mottaret is open from 10:00 am to noon and 2:00 pm to 7:00 pm. Equipment loan and instruction are available.

Boating - Paddle boats, row boats and canoes are available for rent on Lake Tuéda.

Bowling - A six-lane bowling alley is located inside the ice rink building. It is open from 11:00 am to 2:00 am; shoe rentals are available.

Fishing - There is excellent fishing in Lake Tuéda which is allowed on Wednesdays, Sundays and holidays, as well as in local rivers. Fishing permits are on sale at the Tourist Office.

Fitness Centers - The **Aspen Club** is open daily from 9:00 am to midnight. You can receive a 20% reduction on services with the Multi-Activity Card, including therapeutic baths, massage, shiatsu, sauna, jacuzzi, beauty parlour, swimming pool, gym, aerobics, yoga, and more. It is located in the Aspen Park Hotel, tel: 79-00-51-77. **Centre Ludicur** is open daily from 4:00 pm to 8:00 pm in the Hotel la Chaudanne with squash, jacuzzi, sauna, steam, weights, gym, beauty care, massage, and therapeutic baths; tel: 79-08-89-08 for costs and reservations. **Altiport Fitness** at the Altiport Hotel offers sauna, jaccuzzi, gymnasium, massage and solarium; tel: 79-00-52-32. **Le Hameau Fitness Center** is located in Méribel-Mottaret, high above Méribel Centre, and is open from 5:00 pm to 8:00 pm, closed on Saturdays; call 79-00-46-46 for rates and information.

Fitness Parcours - An exercise trail is marked in the forest near the Altiport.

Golf - Golf is available at the Golf Club Méribel, designed on a plateau at the foot of the Dent de Burgin. Forests line the fairways and there are spectacular views of the valley—especially the surrounding alps at hole #12. An established handicap is required to play the course. The club also offers a practice range, putting green, chipping green and two practice bunkers. Call 79-00-50-00 for information and reservations.

Horseback Riding - Check with the riding club of Bois d'Arbin, for lessons for all levels, tel: 79-08-55-09. Ranch Pascal is high up at la Traye at 5578 ft. (1700 m.). Discover the mountains on horseback and spend the night in a mountain hut; tel: 79-00-50-99 for information and costs.

Ice Skating - This indoor rink was used for the 1992 Olympic Ice Hockey tournaments. There is public skating daily from 5:00 pm to 8:00 pm, and additionally Monday, Wednesday and Friday from 9:00 pm to 10:30 pm. Skate rentals are available.

Mini-golf - Available in the Méribel-Mottaret and la Chaudanne areas.

Mountain Biking - Half-day rides with a guide are available. Call VTT Concept in les Allues at 79-08-50-31.

Paragliding - Clinics are available for everyone from beginners to experts; call 79-08-64-81 for information.

Rafting - Daily rafting expeditions take place on the Doron of Bozel. Contact the Tourist Office for more information.

Scenic Flights - Explore the Three Valleys and Mont Blanc—taking off from the Altiport with Méribel Air. A minimum of two passengers is required.

Swimming - The indoor pool is at la Chaudanne and is open weekdays from noon to 7:45 pm, and on weekends from 11:00 am to 7:45 pm. A ten-entrance card is available at a discount.

Tennis - 12 courts are located at Bois d'Arbin; six courts are in Méribel/Mottaret; two courts are at the Altiport; and one court is in les Allues. A discount is available with the Multi-Activities Card. Call the Tennis Club at 79-08-50-04 for reservations.

Excursions in and around Méribel

This section introduces day-excursions that *Easy Walkers* will enjoy when an alternative to walking is desired. Be sure to check current timetables for best connections if public transportation is used.

1. Cable Lifts in Méribel

A) Télécabine de Tougnète - This gondola, rising up to 7874 ft. (2400 m.), runs several times a week in summer— Mondays and Thursdays and every other Friday—but be sure to check with the Tourist Office for current schedules. It is located in the Chaudanne area near the ice rink and is open from 8:30 am to 12:30 pm and 1:45 pm to 5:00 pm, with a mid-station stop, if desired. (See Walk #1 for more details.)

Directions: Take the Méribus and get off at the ice rink. Walk up to the gondola station.

B) Télécabine Burgin-Saulire - This gondola goes to la Saulire peak at 8859 ft. (2700 m.) on Wednesday, the day the Pas du Lac gondola does not run. It leaves from la Chaudanne, next to the Tougnète cable station, and runs from 8:30 am to 12:30 pm and 1:45 pm to 5:00 pm.

Directions: Take the Méribus and get off at the ice rink. Walk up to the station.

C) Télécabine Mont Vallon - This gondola also operates one day a week—on Wednesdays from 10:30 am to 3:30 pm. A three-hour walk into the Vanoise National Park is required to reach this lift, but the views from the peak of Mont Vallon at 9679 ft. (2950 m.) into the unspoiled wilderness of the Vanoise are worth the effort. (See Walk #4 for more details and directions.)

D) Télécabine du Pas-du-Lac - This gondola rises to 8859 ft. (2700 m.) and runs Tuesdays and Thursdays and every other Friday from 8:30 am to 12:30 pm and 2:00 pm to 5:30 pm, but remember to confirm operating days with the Tourist Office. (See Walks #2 and #3 for more details.)

Directions: Take the Méribus to the Mottaret area and exit at the lift station.

> ☞ **HINT: Cable lifts do not operate every day or on weekends in the summer, so walkers should be very careful in selecting the day for a particular hike. We strongly suggest checking days and hours of operation with the Tourist Office and provide a recommended daily schedule in the "Walks" section of this chapter.**

The cost is the same for all lifts: 46 FF for a round-trip ticket (you are actually paying for the ascent, the descent is free), and **cable cars are free if you are 80 years or older!** A pass to use all cable cars for one week, Monday through Friday, is available at a cost of 120 FF, and a photo ID is required. A one-day pass is a good option if you are taking the Courchevel excursion, cost: 64 FF. This pass allows one-day access to **all** lifts open in Courchevel and Méribel.

2. Tuéda Natural Reserve - Created in 1994, this nature area within the Vanoise National Park reaches from Lake Tuéda to the Gebroulaz Glacier via the Refuge des Saut. Along the banks of the Doron River, it comprises 2700 acres (1100 hectares) of natural beauty and unspoiled wilderness. A marked botanical trail will allow *Easy Walkers* to discover over 80 species of alpine flowers and plants, including the rare Cembra pine. (See Walks #4 and #5 for more details.)

Directions: Take the Méribus to the parking lot outside the reserve, in the Mottaret area of Méribel.

3. Vanoise National Park - Situated between the upper valleys of the Tarentaise and Maurienne, the park's mountains and glaciers reach elevations from 4101 ft. (1250 m.) to 12,638 ft. (3852 m.) at the summit of the Grande Casse. The Vanoise and neighboring Gran Paradiso National Park in Italy together form the largest nature reserve in Western Europe. More than a thousand different varieties of flowers can be found in the park, which also boasts the largest herd of ibex in France and over 4500 chamois. Smaller mammals include the hare and marmot, with bird species represented by golden eagles, ptarmigan, black grouse and partridge.

Vanoise includes 310 miles (500 km) of marked trails (access into the park is only by foot), with an exceptional richness of protected flora and fauna. There is also a network of long hikes over mountain passes with reserved lodging available in one of 28 park *refuges*. Check in at the National

Park counter at the Méribel Tourist Office for a slide show and reservations for organized trips into the park.

Directions: The free, convenient Méribus provides regular trips to the park; check at the Tourist Office for its schedule.

4. Chamonix - This world capital of mountaineering is dominated by the majesty of Mont Blanc, the highest mountain in Europe—but the town successfully combines the boutiques, restaurants, hotels and services of a large resort with the incomparable, awesome natural surroundings of the French Alps. (See the "Chamonix" chapter for further details.)

Directions: By car - Drive into Moûtiers, watching for signs for the N90 to Albertville. In Albertville, pick up N212 north through Mègeve, then D909 into St. Gervais, following signs into Chamonix.

5. Albertville - See "Mègeve," Excursion #5.

Directions: By car - Take the main road to Moûtiers, picking up N90 and following the signed directions to Albertville and Conflans.

6. Courchevel - The Saint-Bon Valley developed into one of the world's prime ski centers after World War I with the creation of Courchevel, and area planners decided to develop and expand winter sports to allow Courchevel to compete at the same level as other great European resorts of the era—Davos, Cortina, etc. The Tovets mountainside, with north-facing slopes for consistent snow quality, on a sun-filled plateau, was the stage for the building of the Courchevels. Each of the three areas—Courchevel 1300 (le Praz), Courchevel 1550 and Courchevel 1850—are referred to by the altitude in meters of each town.

Although its origins were simple—in Savoyard *vel* means cows, and *écorché* is the place where cows were killed and skinned—Courchevel 1850 attracts the ultra-rich, ski jet-set and is an important link in the Three Valleys. However, in summer, cows in the mountain pastures around Courchevel still produce almost a thousand wheels of rich Beaufort cheese, the region's main natural resource, and local wood-workers still carve the Saint-Bon style of furniture—rustic, solid and decorated with gometric patterns—mostly from the famous pine of the Arolles.

Easy Walkers might enjoy taking the lift up from Méribel to la Saulire to enjoy the magnificent views of the snow-capped peaks of the French Alps; from there a cable car and gondola then descend to Courchevel 1850. (See Walks #2 and #3 for more details.)

Directions: By car - Drive to Moûtiers and follow signs to the Courchevels.

7. Val d'Isère - See "Bourg-Saint-Maurice/Les Arcs," Excursion #3.

Directions: By car - Drive to Moûtiers and follow signs to N90 and Bourg-St-Maurice. Just past Bourg-St. Maurice turn right on D902 and head southeast to Tignes and Val d'Isère.

8. Annecy - See "Chamonix," Excursion #4.

Directions: By car - Drive to Moûtiers and follow the signs to N90 and Albertville, where you pick up N212 going north. At Ugine, take N508 past Faverge, around the left side of the lake to Annecy.

9. Belleville Valley Towns - See "Bourg-Saint-Maurice/Les Arcs," Excursion #7.

Directions: By car - Drive into Moûtiers and follow signs to the Belleville Valley, driving through the towns of St-Martin-de-Belleville, les Menuires and, finally, Val-Thorens.

10. Chambéry - This beautiful city of 96,000 inhabitants is called the historic capital of the Savoie region. From 1295

to 1536, Chambéry was the capital of a sovereign state stretching from Bern to Nice and Lyons to Turin, and its past lingers in the quaint, old streets of the historic old town. On Saturdays you can visit an open-air market in the **Place de Genève**.

Walk along the pedestrian streets in the renovated old part of the city, near the famous **Elephant Fountain**, or the **Carré Curial** shopping center located in an old barracks dating from Napoleon's time. The **Musée Savoisien** contains archaeological treasures from prehistoric sites around Lake Bourget; the **Musée des Beaux-Arts** has one of the finest collections of Italian paintings in France; the **Musée des Charmettes** is the country house where Jean-Jacques Rousseau lived from 1732 to 1742; and the **Musée d'Histoire Naturelle** contains natural history exhibits.

Directions: By car - Drive into Moûtiers, following signs to Albertville where you pick up A430 and then A43 into Chambéry.

11. Aix-les-Bains and Lac du Bourget - Aix is the second-largest town in the Savoie and the premier spa in France, stretching down to the shores of Lake Bourget, the largest natural lake in France. Stroll in Aix's charming old town and gardens. Many traces of the town's ancient past have been preserved: the **Roman Arch of Campanus**, the **Roman baths**, the **Temple of Diana**, and the **Archaeological Museum** with fine Roman remains and statuary. Visit the **Musée Faure**, containing sculptures by Rodin and a fine collection of impressionist paintings, and stop by the **Aquarium** and **Maison du Lac** on the waterfront.

Boat trips on the lake can take you to the **Savières Canal** or **Hautecombe Abbey**, founded in 1101 by the Benedictine monks, where the Princes of Savoie are entombed. If you are driving around the lake, visit the 11th-century priory at **Le Bourget-du-Lac**, and drive through the famous

Chautagne vineyards, or to **Mont Revard** for breathtaking views over the lake.

Directions: By car - Drive into Moûtiers, following N90 into Albertville where you pick up A430 south, then take A43 past Chambéry into Aix.

12. Bus Tours - The Transavoie bus company runs excursions from Méribel to many interesting villages and areas if you prefer not to drive. They include Annecy, Beaufort, Chamonix, Chartreuse, Hautecombe, Megève, Mont Blanc, Pralognan, Val d'Isère, Vercors and Yvoire/Genève. Check at the Tourist Office for days of departure, length of trips and costs.

Méribel Walks

Recommended Maps:
1) Cartes IGN, #3534 OT - Les Trois Vallées, Modane
2) Carte des Sentiers de Méribel, published by the Méribel Tourist Office

Considering that lifts in the Méribel valley **do not operate every day in summer**, you might wish to use the following schedule of walks if the weather cooperates. However, check with the Tourist Office to confirm days of lift operation and adjust your walking plans accordingly.

Monday: Walk #1 - Tougnete lift.

Tuesday: Walk #2 or Walk #3 - Pas du Lac/Courchevel lifts

Wednesday: Walk #4 - Mont Vallon lift.

Thursday: Walk #5 - Pas du Lac lift.

Friday: Open. Check the "Excursions" section for possible activities. (Pas du Lac lift alternates with the Tougnete lift on Fridays—the Courchevel lift, however, does not operate).

Saturday: Walk #6 (no lift required).

Sunday: Open. Check the "Excursions" section for some suggested destinations.

Walk #1: Lift to Tougnete, Walk to Méribel-Mottaret

Walking Easy Time
3 hours

Easy Walkers will see the best view of the Méribel valley from the peak station of the Tougnete gondola lift. Try to make this excursion when the weather is clear, keeping in mind that this lift operates twice a week, on Monday and Thursday—please check with the Tourist Office before planning this walk. There are facilities at the lift stations but the restaurants are not open, so it might be advisable to pack a picnic lunch.

You will leave from la Chaudanne, a minute or two south of Méribel Centre, near the Olympic Ice Arena, for a "bubble" gondola ride to the Tougnete top station at 7973 ft. (2430 m.). The top station has fabulous views of the Méribel area and the adjacent valley, including the old village of St.-Martin-de-Belleville and the famous ski resort of les Menuires, all leading to ski heaven—Val-Thorens.

The day we visited the Tougnete peak, the famous Tour de France bicycle race was ending one of its sections in Val Thorens and hundreds of people were walking and biking down into this high mountain village to watch the bikers finish their arduous day! From this vantage point you will be able to understand better the importance of ski development in the Méribel Valley. This was the site of the 1992 Winter Olympics' downhill skiing events, and this mountain range is the center of the Trois Vallées, providing winter skiing for up to 220,000 skiers per hour.

After exploring the opportunities along the ridge of Tougnete towards the Pas de Cherferie, *Easy Walkers* will return to the downhill jeep road near the Tougnete peak and descend past the mid-station for the gentle walk to Méribel-Mottaret and the Méribus return.

Directions: Take the free, convenient Méribus to the Olympic Ice Rink at la Chaudanne and the Tougnete gondola lift—a few minute walk. Buy a one-way ticket to the top, taking the two-section gondola to the peak.

Start: After enjoying the views, explore the ridge trail descending towards Pas de Cherferie. Walk only as long as you are comfortable, remembering that you will be returning to the jeep road (ascending back towards the Tougnete peak) to begin today's walk.

From the top station, take the jeep road down on your left, on a zig-zag path. Stay to the left at the first intersection, passing under a ski lift and turning right at the next intersection in the direction of the mid-station. At the mid-station, circle around and underneath the gondola cars, staying on the jeep road to the right in the direction of Mottaret. Stay to your right, not descending on the car road, but walk-

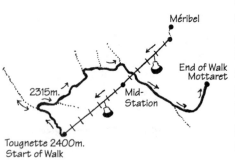

ing along the mountain under several more ski lifts and towards the Chalets du Mottaret. A left turn brings you down to the large parking lot. A right turn takes you up along a route above Lake Tuéda, where you can then turn down a zig-zagging path to the end of the lake and walk back along the lake to the parking lot and the Méribus stop for the return.

Walk #2: Méribel-Mottaret Pas du Lac Lift to La Saulire, Lift Down to Courchevel, Walk Courchevel 1850 to Méribel Altiport

Walking Easy Time
2½ hours

Reserve the better part of the day for a series of high-mountain lifts to the internationally famous ski resort of Courchevel 1850. Pack your picnic lunch for today's excursion, although there are some limited restaurant options in Courchevel. You will take a gondola from Mottaret to the peak station of la Saulire at 8859 ft. (2700 m.), for a 360-degree panorama of the surrounding peaks.

After descending to Courchevel on a giant, 160-passenger capacity, cable car, you'll transfer to a gondola for the final descent to Courchevel 1850, the beginning of today's walk. Courchevel 1850 is a modern ski center, built in the 1950s to service winter sports enthusiasts. It is a mix of concrete condominiums, apartments and hotels, mostly closed in summer, although there are some interesting walks in the beautiful surrounding mountains. Courchevel 1850 overlooks Courchevel 1650 and the more traditional villages of le Praz and St. Bon.

Directions: Take the 9:25 or 9:55 am Méribus to the Pas du Lac lift station in Méribel-Mottaret. Purchase a 64 FF one-day lift pass, entitling you to unlimited lifts in the area for today. Take the gondola to the top station, remaining in the four-passenger gondola as you pass through the mid-station and showing your ticket to the attendant. Exit at la Saulire and enjoy the incredible vista of the snow-covered peaks, many in the Vanoise National Park.

When ready, walk up to the Courchevel-la Saulire lift station for the four-minute descent to the mid-station on the giant cable car. Change to a modern, eight-passenger gondola for the short ride to Courchevel 1850. Exit, walking to your left for a visit to the Office of Tourism in the building underneath the lift station.

Start: Turn left on leaving the building, passing several large hotels as you descend on the wide auto road to its termination at a paved circle and ski lift. Take the **unmarked** gravel path to the left in the direction of the forest, where the path will narrow to a comfortable wagon path. A sign indicates the path is for cross-country skiing, and while it says "not for walking," those directions are for winter only. For the remainder of this walk, stay on the main wagon path in the direction of Méribel.

In a few minutes another sign indicates the path to Plantrey and Bouc Blanc with another not-so-timely warning, "Be careful, you are crossing a major alpine run, give way to the skiers!" Little chance of skiers now, however, so continue ahead. Note the superb views of small villages and hamlets dotting the valley and mountains on the right; there are side

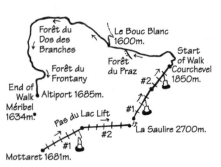

paths that can tempt you into the forest, but remain on the major trail. After a while, signs confirm your direction to Méribel.

It is interesting to note that you will be walking through three forests on your way from Courchevel to Méribel/Altiport. The first is Forêt du Praz, and it takes about 45 minutes to exit the forest onto a nice open meadow lined with wildflowers. Continue ahead, meeting a signed junction for le Bouc-Blanc, and a trail going up to the left to Lac Bleu, but forge ahead on the main path, following the signs for Méribel.

You now enter the second forest, Forêt du Dos des Branches, where the road eventually divides. Follow the path up to the left, ascending gently in the direction of Méribel. This trail is now blazed regularly with yellow dots. The golf course at Altiport appears through the trees on the right, and while it is possible to take a steep mountain path to Altiport on the left, do **not** take that trail, but remain on the main path, following additional Altiport signs all the way to a paved auto road.

Easy Walkers have two options to catch the Méribus back to their hotel. If you turn left and walk up the paved road, you will reach the Altiport, the Altiport Hotel, the Golf Course, and the bus stop in the parking lot in front of the hotel. The second option for *Easy Walkers* as you meet the paved auto road is to make a right turn down to the restaurant le Blanchot and another bus stop (*arret navette*). Check the bus schedule and, if there is time, enjoy the sun terrace of the restaurant, overlooking the golf course.

Walk #3: Méribel-Mottaret Pas du Lac Lift to La Saulire, Lift to Courchevel Mid-Station, Walk to Courchevel 1850, Lift to La Saulire, Walk to Mottaret

Walking Easy Time
2½ to 4 hours

Today's walk utilizes a combination of lift systems, interspersed with downhill walking. It also affords *Easy Walkers*

the opportunity of viewing the Méribel Valley, Méribel-Mottaret, and Courchevel 1850. There are a few conditions you should think about before setting off, however. First, confirm with the Tourist Office that the Saulire and Courchevel lifts are operating on the same day. This usually occurs on Tuesdays and Thursdays in summer, but is of course, subject to change. Second, you may not wish to visit Courchevel again if you are planning to take Walk #2. And of course, the weather should be sunny and clear, as we recommend for all high-level excursions.

You will take the Pas du Lac lift from Méribel-Mottaret at 5515 ft. (1681 m.) to the peak of la Saulire at 8859 ft. (2700 m.). Here you will find fabulous views over Courchevel and the Vanoise National Park, including Mont du Vallon at 9686 ft. (2952 m.), towered over by the Aiguille de Péclet at 11,684 ft. (3561 m.) that looks down on the famous ski resort of Val-Thorens. In the other direction, the Glacier de la Vanoise is bordered by the Aiguille du Fruit at 10,010 ft. (3051 m.), and below them lies the internationally renowned ski resort of Courchevel 1850—today's destination.

From the peak at la Saulire you will descend to the Courchevel mid-station and walk down to Courchevel 1850. After visiting this resort, you will return to la Saulire using the gondola and cable car. *Easy Walkers* now have the option of walking back to Mottaret, a descent of 3281 ft. (1000 m.), on a well-graded, open, jeep road, or taking the gondola back to the Pas du Lac mid-station, for the easy walk to Mottaret, picking up the same jeep trail.

Directions: Take the free Méribus, getting off at the Pas du Lac lift station at Mottaret. Purchase a one-day Méribel lift pass and take the gondola to la Saulire top station. Stay in the gondola as you pass through the mid-station, showing the ticket to the attendant. After taking in the spectacular panorama, walk up to the Courchevel cable car station and take the large, 160-passenger cable car to Courchevel mid-station, les Verdons at 6815 ft. (2077 m.).

Start: Exit the mid-station and walk to your left on a well-graded path, passing your first right turn and walking down by and under two ski lifts to the bend in the road. A forest trail will take you straight ahead into Courchevel 1850. If you wish, you can stay on the road as it zig-zags to the little lake and golf course on your right, continuing to walk into Courchevel from there. Courchevel 1850 is not a particularly pretty village in summer, but you might enjoy having lunch or browsing through the shops in town. This village was built primarily to accommodate the tens of thousands of winter visitors who come to the area for out-standing skiing. When ready, take the modern, eight-pas-senger Verdons gondola back to the mid-station and change for the large cable car up to la Saulire.

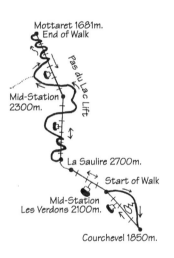

Option 1) *Easy Walkers* can descend to Mottaret by walking down the wide jeep trail, past the mid-station. Go left at the fork in the road at 7136 ft. (2175 m.), zig-zagging down to Méribel-Mottaret and the main road. This is a de-scent of a little over 3281 ft. (1000 m.), and you should stop and rest your knees on occasion.

Option 2) Your second option is to take the Pas du Lac gondola to the mid-station and walk down to Mottaret from there. The descent from the mid-station is only 1969 ft. (600 m.). Access to the path down to Mottaret is to the left as you exit the mid-station. Make your first left at the fork in the road, continuing down to Mottaret on the wide jeep trail, through open meadows ablaze with white, yellow, purple and lavender flowers, with the wooden chalets of Mottaret and the Olympic ski slopes on the opposite side of the valley visible at all times. At the main road, take the Méribus to the stop closest to your hotel.

Walk #4: Méribel-Mottaret into the Vanoise National Park to Mont Vallon Lift to Méribel-Mottaret (Excursion to Mont Vallon)

Walking Easy Time
5 hours

A full day's excursion is in store for *Easy Walkers* today, but it must be carefully planned, as the remote Mont Vallon gondola lift only operates one day per week, usually on a Wednesday. Please check with the Méribel Tourist Office for the day of operation and weather conditions. Even on a clear day, make sure you pack your insulated jacket, as the temperature at the peak will be at the freezing point. There are limited facilities and no food is available on today's hike, so pack a picnic lunch and, of course, water.

The walk to Mont Vallon is rated "more challenging," but it is well within the range of those in good physical shape. There is **no** difficult or perilous walking involved, but the altitude increases from 5591 ft. (1704 m.) to 7051 ft. (2149 m.)—a rise of 1460 ft. (445 m.)—on a wide jeep road. The return is a delightful descent along the same path. This is the only route available to reach the Mont Vallon gondola lift, and it takes about three hours for the ascent. Yet this is one of the most popular hikes in the Vanoise National Park, and on a clear day, about 750 walkers take this hike in order to take the gondola to Mt. Vallon.

The Vanoise was developed to preserve and protect the upper valleys of the Tarentaise region, encompassing many mountains over 9843 ft. (3000 m.) and numerous glaciers. Preserves within the park are reserved for the protection of nature without the intrusion of civilization, except for the mountain *refuges*. In winter, skiers enjoy the natural environment, but leave the reserve at the end of the day.

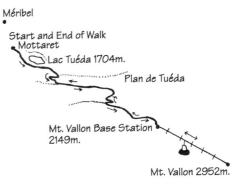

While the walk up to Mont Vallon takes about three hours, with an almost two-hour return, the real treat in store for *Easy Walkers* is the view from the top of Mont du Vallon at 9653 ft. (2942 m.). This is the highest viewing point we take you to in the mountains surrounding Méribel, and on a clear day you can see Mont Blanc as well as every major peak and glacier in the Three Valleys. The walk back is along the same path, passing Lac Tuéda, for the return to Mottaret.

Directions: Take the 9:25 am Méribus leaving from the Hotel Allodis (or other convenient locations) for the ride to the Mottaret-Lac Tuéda parking lot. Of course, if you have your own car, there is plenty of available parking at the entrance to the Tuéda Preserve. Follow the signs to Mottaret and Lac de Tuéda for the short drive from Méribel.

Start: Walk through the parking lot and onto a wide plain, passing to the right side of Lac Tuéda. At the end of the little lake, a trail ascends to the right, passing a small dairy farm where local cheeses are produced and sold. You will ascend from 5591 ft. (1704 m.) at the lake to 5906 ft. (1800 m.) to reach the main path going directly to the Mont Vallon lift. This very popular path is well-marked with signs to Mont Vallon and climbs up to the lift station at 7051 ft. (2149 m.)—take the ascent very slowly and rest as often as needed.

At the lift station, buy a round-trip ticket for a thrilling seven-minute gondola ascent to the peak station at 9686 ft. (2952 m.). This is the time to put on your warm jacket as the temperatures are usually below freezing. Sensational views of the glaciers of the Vanoise, as well as high peaks in all directions, will have made the uphill hike worthwhile.

When ready, return to the base station for the walk back along the same trail, this time descending pleasantly, with views of Lac Tuéda. The return hike to the parking lot or bus stop should take less than two hours.

Walk #5: Lift to Pas du Lac Mid-Station, Walk to Chalet du Fruit to Lac Tuéda to Méribel-Mottaret (with possible extension to Refuge du Saut)

Walking Easy Time
3½ to 6 hours

Today's more aggressive hike begins from the mid-station of the Pas du Lac lift in Mottaret and enters the Tuéda Reserve in the Vanoise National Park in the direction of Refuge du Saut. *Easy Walkers* have the option of descending down and around to Chalet du Fruit at 6004 ft. (1830 m.)

or taking the extension past Chalet de la Plagne all the way to Refuge du Saut at 6956 ft. (2120 m.) and returning on the same trail, then descending to Chalet du Fruit down through Plan de Tuéda, past the lake, into Mottaret. It is possible to take this hike starting from the lake, ascending past the Chalet du Fruit and on to the *refuge*, but the climb up to the chalet may be a bit steep, although it can be handled if done slowly. At any rate, we have suggested taking it from the mid-station of the Pas du Lac lift, avoiding the climb past the Chalet du Fruit. Pack your lunch and water, of course.

Directions: Take the Méribus to the Pas du Lac lift station in Mottaret. Purchase a one-way ticket to the mid-station and exit there.

Start: Turn left as you exit the station and locate the jeep road descending down the mountain. Walk under the lift, and then under one ski lift down to a second ski lift, where the trail continues into the meadows and up to the left. This is where you depart from the road, following the sign to Refuge du Saut. Do **not** walk down the road

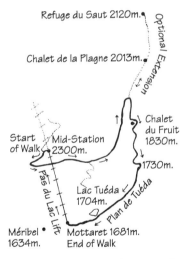

to Mottaret. This trail continues up through the meadows and forest until it meets the wider path descending to Chalet du Fruit. If you choose to take the extended hike to Refuge du Saut, continue down the road for a minute or two, following the sign to the left, past Chalet de la Plagne, up to the Refuge du Saut at 6961 ft. (2126 m.). If you take this extension, remember, you can reverse your direction at any time. This is a rather long hike and you should feel fit before taking it.

If you choose not to take the extension, continue down the road, taking the rather steep but manageable descent, past Chalet du Fruit into Plan de Tuéda. Walk past the lake to the parking area and the Méribus.

Walk #6: Les Allues to Le Villaret to Hauteville to Villarnard to Hauteville to Les Allues

 Walking Easy Time
3½ to 4 hours

Our walk today begins in the lower Méribel Valley in its main village of les Allues, a four-mile (6-km) drive from Méribel. The word *allues* dates back to the 13th century, when the inhabitants of the area were exempted from local taxes, becoming known as freeholders, or *allodis* in the old French language. The church in this village dates back to the 17th century and is dedicated to St. Martin, patron saint of the village.

Walkers will descend on a narrow path, over a rushing stream, to the stone remains of an ancient mill. There is the option to continue up to le Villaret and take the quiet, country road to Hauteville, or to ascend to Hauteville through the forest on a steeper path. A forest path takes you around the mountain, ascending and descending to the hamlet of Villarnard. You will return along the same path, but once on the road at Hauteville, you can stay on this quiet road all the way back to les Allues.

This will be a picnic lunch day as there are no restaurants or facilities between the beginning and end of the hike.

Directions: While it is possible to take a bus to les Allues, we recommend that you use your car for today's excursion, as bus times may not coincide with your return. Drive from Méribel down to les Allues at 3708 ft. (1130 m.) and park in any available spot in the area of the church, which is usually open for visits on Wednesday afternoons only.

Start: Walk back to the main road on the little road you entered les Allues on, passing the tennis court on your left. Cross the road and walk a minute to your right to the sign for le Villaret and Hauteville. Follow the descending path on the left down through a small suburban area. Continue descending under a ski lift, heading towards the rushing water below, and cross on a small wooden bridge. After crossing the bridge you will see the stone remains of an old mill. A sign a few feet

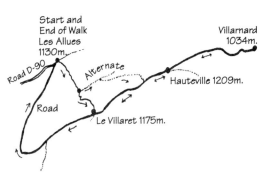

ahead will direct you to the right to le Villaret. This path takes you up through woods and meadows to the hamlet of le Villaret at 3855 ft. (1175 m.) and a paved country road. Make a left turn on the road in the direction of Hauteville.

It is also possible, from the point after the bridge crossing, to take a short cut by walking to your left to Hauteville on a rocky, descending trail, but walkers who choose this trail will then have to find an **unsigned**, steep path rising up the mountain into the forest on their right. This trail meets the country auto road before Hauteville.

At 3967 ft. (1209 m.) in Hauteville the road ends. Take the left path through the woods in the direction of Villarnard. The path rolls around and down the mountain to the hamlet of Villarnard at 3393 ft. (1034 m.). When ready, return on the same path to Hauteville and take the quiet, country road through le Villaret, all the way down to les Allues, where you parked your car.

EMBRUN

Embrun, one of the most important resort villages in the Hautes-Alpes, sits high on a rocky terrace overlooking the Durance River and Lake Serre-Ponçon, the largest man-made lake in Europe. Once a "cathedral city," Embrun now attracts large numbers of water-sport enthusiasts, walkers and campers during the high season of July and August, bringing tourism dollars into what used to be a somewhat disadvantaged valley. The 20-mile-long lake was formed when the Durance river bed was dammed in the 1950s and spreads over 75,000 acres. The lake, surrounding mountains and charming, neighboring villages make the Embrunais (the area around Embrun) an unusually attractive *Walking Easy* destination.

Embrun is the nucleus of activities within the Embrunais and the gateway to the wilderness of Parc Nature Régional du Queyras and the famous peaks of Parc National des Ecrins. Embrun has the distinct advantage of being close to a multitude of activities—from water sports on Lake Serre-Ponçon to a myriad of walks in the mountains and meadows to the ski resorts of les Orres and Réallon.

As you expand the perimeter around Embrun, the high peak and imposing glacier of la Meije at 13,068 ft. (3983 m.) in the Ecrins Park; the natural beauty of the Queyras Park, the setting of Saint-Véran, Europe's highest village; the fabulous, desert-like mountain crossing over Col d'Izoard at 7874 ft. (2400 m.), ringed by dramatic peaks; and ancient Briançon, the highest small city in Europe at 4334 ft. (1321 m.) are all easily reached. You have the best of all sporting, cultural, and walking worlds around the *Walking Easy* base village of Embrun.

Embrun is a secret jewel of the French Alps, waiting to be discovered by American and English walkers. One can't help but sense its prestigous past when walking through this well-maintained town—the colorful, narrow streets lined with boutiques and charming cafés. A portion of Embrun's heritage is revealed in a walk from the centrally located Tourist Office to the finest cathedral in the southern Alps, dating back to the end of the 12th century, and the fountains, arched doorways and stone sculptures on Embrun's cobblestone streets reflect its architectural importance. The well-organized Tourist Office is situated at the head of Embrun's walking streets, in the extraordinary and historically important Gothic chapels of an ancient convent, with recently restored 15th- and 16th-century frescoes.

Located south of Grenoble, Embrun is close to the Italian border, not far from Marseilles and the French Riviera. This region is a mix of Dauphinois and Provençal—with fields of lavender alpine flowers and Mediterranean sunshine warming the fresh, cool mountain air. The Hautes-Alpes has a population of only 113,000 in 2180 square miles (5643 sq. km), and altitudes rise from 1640 ft. (500 m.) at Buëch to 13,458 ft. (4102 m.) on the Barre des Ecrins. In remote Hautes-Alpes villages, *Easy Walkers* may still hear dialects with roots tracing back to the ancient Oc language of southern France:

English	**French**	**Dialect**
sunshine	*soleil*	*cagnard*
street	*rue*	*charriere*
road	*chemin*	*draille*
face	*visage*	*moure*
more	*encore, plus*	*maí*
cold wind	*vent froid*	*rispe*
seat	*siège*	*seti*

Look for ancient sundials as you travel through the Hautes-Alpes—through Pays de Buëch, the Queyras, the Valloise, and the Briançon areas. Created to keep time for the villagers, these unique artistic and cultural timepieces have survived since their inceptions in the 18th century. (See Walk #6 for details on the sundials in Saint-Véran.)

Embrun has exceptionally beautiful surroundings—old, fortified ramparts high above the valley, a majestic cathedral, ancient buildings and stone sculptures—all surrounded by meadows, farms and sleepy country hamlets. You will be astonished at the charm and vitality of this off-the-beaten-path village and its *Walking Easy* trails.

Transportation to Embrun

By Plane: There is an international airport at Nice, on the Côte d'Azur, with a change of plane in Paris, if you fly into France from the United States. Flying into Geneva will also entail a change of plane, as well as a longer drive than from Nice.

By Train: Two main rail lines from Paris and Marseilles provide daily service to Briançon by way of Gap. A Bi-Pass ticket is available on these lines, and the price and reservation include train, plus bus or taxi transfer to Embrun. Trains from Paris and Marseilles are also scheduled into the Gare S.N.C.F. à Embrun, the station at Embrun.

By Car: From Nice by car, take N202 north and then west to N85 to Digne-les-Bains, picking up D900. When D900 forks at the lake, take the right fork of D900 a short distance, driving left (north) around the lake to Embrun. From Geneva, take N201 south, picking up superhighway E712 north of Annecy to bypass the urban area and continuing on E712 south to Grenoble. Follow D5 south to N85 south into Gap, and N94 east into Embrun.

From south of Grenoble, pick up N85 to Gap, the Route Napoléon. This scenic road runs from the Mediterranean Sea at Golfe-Juan to Grenoble, following the route taken by Napoléon on his return from Elba in 1832. It is marked on its entire length by the flying eagle symbol, inspired by Napoléon's remark, "The eagle will fly from steeple to steeple until he reaches the towers of Notre-Dame." In Gap, pick up N94 east into Embrun.

From Marseille, take expressway A51 around Aix-en-Provence to above Sisteron, where you pick up N85 to Gap, then N94 east to Embrun. Coming from the Briançon area, take N94 south into Embrun.

Note: It is necessary to have the use of a car while in Embrun for transportation to and from walks and sightseeing!

Activities in Embrun

This section lists activities available in Embrun on days when additions or alternatives to walking are desired. The historic Office de Tourisme de L'Embrunais, headed by the interesting and charming director Mme. Claude Chowanietz, is on Place Général Dosse, tel: 92-43-01-80.

Boating - Check with the Tourist Office for current details on the availability at Lake Serre-Ponçon.

Fishing - The Tourist Office can provide fishing licenses and details on Lake Serre-Ponçon.

Swimming - The municipal swimming pool in Plan d'Eau is open every day from 10:00 am to 7:00 pm and swimming is also permitted at the lake.

Excursions in and around Embrun

This section introduces day excursions that *Easy Walkers* will enjoy when an alternative to walking is desired.

1. Lifts around Embrun

A) Les Orres - During the summer, three chairlifts operate in les Orres: Prélongis, rising to 6316 ft. (1925 m.), operating every day; Fontaines, rising to 7901 ft. (2408 m.), open four days a week; and Pousterle, rising to 8301 ft. (2530 m.), open the days Fontaines is closed. Fontaines and Pousterle operate from the top of the Prélongis station. (See Walk #4 for more details.)

Directions: Take the main road past Embrun in the direction of Crots, turning off to Baratier and les Orres at the traffic circle. Do not turn off at les Orres village, but continue driving to les Orres Station.

B) Télésiège de Réallon - This double chairlift operates Monday, Tuesday and Friday in summer (check with the Tourist Office for schedule changes)—from des Aurans to the mid-station and Chabrieres to the top at Belvédère at 7010 ft. (2135 m.). The top station provides spectacular views of the nearby, needle-like Aiguilles de Chabrières. (See Walk #3 for more details.)

Directions: Drive on the main road away from Embrun towards Savines-le-Lac. Cross the bridge and follow the signs to Réallon and then Réallon Station, driving on an ascending, winding mountain road with views of Lake Serre-Ponçon.

2. Boscodon Abbey (Abbaye de Boscodon) - The

12th-century Boscodon Abbey is two miles from Lake Serre-Ponçon and 400 feet above the valley. It is the largest abbey in the region, built by hermit monks of the order of Chalais.

Extensive renovations are taking place, but the abbey church, with its austere lines and somber beauty, can be visited, and it is open every day from 10:00 am to 7:00 pm. An English brochure is available at a nominal cost. (See Walk #2 for more details.)

Directions: Driving past Crots in the direction of Savines-le-Lac, turn at the Boscodon sign and follow the road into the hills.

3. Montdauphin - By command of King Louis XIV, the famous military engineer Vauban ordered the **Fort of Montdauphin** to be built above Guillestre. Wander through narrow streets and visit the craftsmen's shops, constructed of the pink stone peculiar to this area. Nearby, facing Mont Dauphin on the steep rocky slopes above the Durance, an impressive, open-air stalactite formed above a natural basin—it's called the **Petrified Fountain of Réotier**.

Directions: By car - Take N94 north to D902 into Guillestre. Follow local signs to Montdauphin.

4. Briançon - The highest city in Europe, at 4351 ft. (1326 m.), at the crossroads of five valleys and near the Italian border, Briançon's landscape is dominated by its ancient fortifications. The first walls were built in the middle ages, then added to by the military engineer Vauban, turning Briançon into a heavily fortified town. Briançon's narrow streets are filled with small stores and cafés, while in its old quarter, the upper town or **Ville Haute**, the **Church of the Cordelier** entices art lovers with ancient paintings and frescoes. The twin-towered **Eglise Notre-Dame** boasts a lovely view of the surrounding countryside, and the blue-and-white front of the **Pope's House** is a reminder that Italy is not too far away.

Directions: By car - Take N94 north to Briançon.

5. Gap - Situated in a pleasant, glacial valley only 16 miles (26 km) from Embrun, Gap's economy is supported by farms on the surrounding hillsides—it's one of the most prosperous areas in the southern Alps. Visit the **cathedral** and the **museum** and its archeological collection. Outside of town, the **Château de Tallard**, once owned by knights of the Order of Malta, is perched on a rocky outcropping. Note also that this town's Roman origins are still intact and very much in evidence.

The Tourist Office is well organized and they have put together a Randonées Pedestres packet that includes precise instructions for over 20 day walks, mostly blazed, and at all levels of difficulty. Unfortunately, everything is printed in French. If you bone up on your high school French and check the easy-to-follow maps, you might enjoy walking in the Gapençais. It is always a good idea to carry the IGN map of the area as well (#3338 Gap).

Directions: By car - Cross Lake Serre-Ponçon at Savines-le-Lac on route N94 west in the direction of Chorges, and then drive to Gap.

6. La Meije - A two-stage cable car takes you from the tiny village of **la Grave**, with its traditional architecture, up to 10,500 ft. (3200 m.) on the western flank of Mont Rateau and unsurpassed views of 13,065-foot (3982-meter) la Meije and the Ecrins glaciers. In the heart of the Haute Romanche, la Grave, Villar d'Arène and hamlets at even higher levels at the foot of la Meije offer stunning views of the mountain and its glaciers. In summer these impressive glaciers form a fascinating backdrop to the colorful meadow flowers.

Directions: By car - Take N94 to Briançon, then N91 to la Grave.

7. Queyras Regional Park and Villages - A vast, almost forgotten area, this 250 square miles of open alpine country has trails leading through larch woods to higher-elevation pine and grazing sheep amid wildflowers and berries—a visual feast and a photographer's delight. Abriès, Aiguilles, Arvieux, Ceillac, Château-Ville-Vielle, Molines, Ristolas, Saint-Véran—these villages in the highest valley in the Hautes-Alpes enjoy a reputation for wood craftsmanship, since the 16th century when villagers began carving objects during the long winter months. Don't miss the shops of the modern-day wood craftsmen.

At 6693 ft. (2040 m.), Saint-Véran is called "the village where the cocks peck at the stars," the highest village in Europe. It is one of the main tourist attractions of the Queyras, notably for its distinctive, old architecture— wooden buildings decorated with sundials and long galleries where crops are dried. (See Walk #6 for more details.)

Directions: By car - Take N94 north. Turn right on D902 to Guillestre, driving on D902 through the Combe du Queyras to Ville-Vielle. Pick up D5 south to St. Véran.

8. Parc National des Ecrins - Founded in 1973, Ecrins is the largest national park in France, covering over 350 square miles (91,800 hectares). Its 221,000 acres of unspoiled land includes the famous Massif des Ecrins which reaches its high point at the Barre des Ecrins. Bounded by the Romanch, Durance and Drac valleys, the park covers the entire spectrum of spectacular mountain scenery and lies at altitudes between 2625 ft. and 13,459 ft. (800 m. and 4102 m.).

Within the Ecrins' mountain ranges are impressive glaciers—the Glacier Blanc, the Glacier Noir, the Mont-de-Lans and Monétier—and a network of smaller glaciers and mountain lakes. The flora is typical of alpine landscapes and includes several rare species among its 2000 types of flowers. The park's fauna includes most alpine mammals such as chamois, marmots and ermines; 110 different types of birds; and numerous species of insects and invertebrates little-known to the public.

There are about 400 miles of marked trails here, constantly monitored, and the saying in the park is that you'll
meet more chamois than people on the trails! Only one gate
marks the entrance into the park, the narrow road winding
through the Vallée du Guil. The Park House is at Vallouise,
and it offers numerous activities including exhibitions, lectures and discussions, videos, workshops, etc. *Easy Walkers*
can follow the signed path around the house, a walk in a
type of open-air museum, discovering a different way to look
at nature.

Directions: By car - Take N94 towards Briançon. At
l'Argentière-la-Bessée, turn left onto D994 and follow signs
to the Park House Information Center at Vallouise.

9. Les Demoiselles Coiffées - Sometimes called "fairy
chimneys," they are one of the strangest sites in the Hautes-
Alpes, although the authors also encountered these rare
geological formations in the Italian Alps (the Earth Pyramids
of Segonzona). Stony columns of crumbly, alluvial deposits
support enormous rocks at their tops, protecting them from
further erosion.

Directions: By car - Drive past Savines-le-Lac on D954
in the direction of Barcelonnette. There is a parking area
and signs pointing in the direction of the columns, also visible
from sections of the road. You can also see some of these
formations on the ascent to Saint-Véran (see Walk #6 for
more details).

10. Orcières/Merlette - Located at the crossroads of the
Northern Alps and Southern Alps and at the southern end
of Ecrins National Park, Orcières at 4721 ft. (1439 m.) and
its higher neighbor Merlette, 6030 ft. (1838), were fortunate
to inherit an abundance of snow along with bright sunshine,
making this resort an ideal setting for skiers in winter and
walkers in summer.

Directions: By car - Drive N94 west out of town to Gap where you pick up N85 north. At D944, turn right or east and follow the road to the end of the valley. The road splits twice—take the right fork both times to Orciéres.

11. Lake Serre-Ponçon (Lac de Serre-Ponçon) - This body of water is the largest man-made lake in Europe, with 20 miles of crystal-clear water ideal for swimming, fishing, sailing, water skiing, canoeing, and rowing. **Chapelle Saint-Michel** on its tiny island in the lake is the only remnant of the old, drowned village of Savines. A new resort village of Savines-le-Lac was built nearby on the shore of the new lake. The green surrounding mountains contrast pleasantly with the bright blue of the lake, dotted with small sailing boats and wind-surfers.

Directions: By car - Turn left out of town on N94. To drive around the lake, take N94 to D954 south to D900 west, picking up the winding D3 leading to N94 and a right turn to Embrun.

12. Barcelonette - The streets of Barcelonette, population 3314, were laid out in 1213! Many of its ancient buildings are painted in warm colors to counteract the glare of snow and were designed with large projections to protect them from heavy snowfalls. The "Barcelonettes" or "Mexicans," were local townspeople who made fortunes in the textile trade with Mexico in the 1800s. When they returned to Barcelonette they built homes which can still be seen on the outskirts of town.

An interesting side excursion from Barcelonette is the six-mile (10-km) drive northwest on a very winding road to the **Bordoux Torrent (Riou Bordoux)** of the Ubaye Valley, considered by geologists to be a textbook example of erosion in a glacial landscape.

Directions: By car - Take D954 south, picking up D900 east in Le Lauzet-Ubaye to Barcelonnette.

13. Digne-les-Bains - The capital of the so-called "Lavender Alps," or the Alpes de Haute-Provence, Digne is the perfect place to relax in shaded parks and enjoy flowered fountains. Note the old alpine facades of the buildings, combined with the local Provençal charm, and stroll along walking-only streets to shop and relax in the outdoor cafés.

Directions: By car - Take D954 south, picking up D900 west and then south into Digne.

14. Aix-en-Provence - This small city of 130,000 residents has a wonderful mix of good restaurants, chic boutiques, art galleries, cafés, theater and music, and a university—all within a 30-minute walking radius. Aix is close to the sun and sand of Mediterranean beaches and near the summer and winter sports centers of the French Alps. The Tourist Office, off la Rotonde at 2 Pl. du Général-de-Gaulle, is open from 8:00 am to 10:00 pm. Check with them for guided tours in English to Cezanne-related sites. **Sur les Pas de Cezanne**, a walking path through Aix and its suburbs, can be accessed easily via an English brochure available at the Tourist Office.

In the old town, visit **Cathédrale St-Sauveur**, with architectural styles bridging 15 centuries (its baptistry dates from the fourth century!); Romanesque **Cloître St-Sauveur**, a small, 12th-century cloister reached through a door on the right aisle of the cathedral; and the **Musée des Tapisseries**, with rare tapestries, adjoining the cathedral. In July and August the museum's courtyard hosts Aix's music festival. The museum is open from 9:30 am to noon and 2:00 pm to 6:00 pm, closed Tuesday, with an admission charge. Also visit **Musée d'Histoire Naturelle** and its dinosaur egg exhibit at 6 Rue Espariat, open 10:00 am to noon and 2:00 pm to 6:00 pm, closed Sunday morning; admission is charged.

The square, **Place de l'Hôtel de Ville**, is home to a colorful flower market in the morning. Note the 16th-century **clock tower** next to the 17th-century **town hall** with its old wooden doors, wrought-iron balcony and archway. An 18th-century **grain market** building on the south side of the square is now a post office. **Eglise Ste-Marie-Madeleine** on Pl. des Prêcheurs contains a large painting attributed to both Rembrandt and Rubens. Walk uphill at the city's edge to 9 Av. Paul-Cézanne and Cézanne's studio **(Atelier de Cézanne)**. It has been preserved as the artist left it and is open from noon to 2:00 pm daily except Tuesday, with admission charge.

If you have time for shopping in Aix, sample its rich candies—almond paste (*calissons d'Aix*), hazelnut nougat (*victorines*), famous Puyricard chocolates; colorful Provençal fabrics and clothes; and carved, wooden Christmas figures (*santons*).

Directions: Take N94 to Gap, N85 south to expressway A51, then follow signs into the city.

Embrunais Walks

Recommended Maps:
1) IGN 3615 - 3438 ET Top 25, Embrun, Les Orres, Lac de Serre-Ponçon
2) IGN 3437 ET Top 25 - Orcières-Merlette
3) IGN 3637 - Mont Viso, St-Véran, Aiguilles

Walk #1: Introductory Walk in and around Embrun

Walking Easy Time
3 hours

Park your car in the center of Embrun. Walk along the main auto road in the direction of the lake to arrive at a shopping area at the foot of the village. Walk through the parking area and pick up the Moulineaux path, going down along the rock. At the crossroads, turn left, walking along the small, country car road under the rock, with tiny farms on the left and right, until you reach another intersection. Turn left and follow the car road up to town.

This might be a good time to spend the rest of the afternoon acquainting yourself with this fascinating town. The best way to begin is at the Office de Tourisme on Place Général Dosse, in a little square off the main pedestrian shopping street. The Tourist Office headquarters is located in four chapels of the ancient convent of les Cordeliers, consecrated in 1447, and the frescoes in these Gothic chapels have been recently restored—pay the Tourist Office a visit and spend a few minutes admiring the treasures of this ancient building. The director of this office, Madame Claude Chowanietz, heads up an efficient and helpful staff who provide the latest information on cultural, sporting and walking opportunities in the Embrunais.

The ancient city of Embrun, high above the Durance River on its sheer rock cliffs, was named because of its location—from the Celtic *ebr* meaning water and *dunum*, height. During the Roman Empire, Embrun was capital of the Alps region and, until the French Revolution, a fortifed military town. Embrun was also called the "Lourdes of the Middle Ages," as thousands of people made pilgrimages to its famous Gothic cathedral to seek cures for their ailments.

From the Tourist Office walk to rue Clovis Hugues, noting building #29 with seven arcades and a 12th-century sculpted lion. At the top of the street on Place St. Marcellin, beneath a 100-year-old tree is a marble fountain made of stone from Queyras. Walk on to rue Caffe with its overhanging houses and turn right into rue Neuve—on the front of two houses here are 18th-century armorial bearings and an inscription from the 16th century.

In Place Dongois, with its ancient fountain, turn right into rue Isnel to reach 16th-century Place de la Marie. From this square walk down rue Clovis Hugues as far as Place de la Mazelière and note an old tower, a medieval figure on a wall and a fountain monument to those who died in the war of 1870. Continue walking along rue de la Liberté to the former Hotel of Governors, with its Gothic wooden door dating from the Renaissance. Note the lion casting its shadow over the entrance.

At the bottom of rue de la Liberté, turn left into rue Emile Guigues and walk to the cathedral bell tower at the end of the street. As you walk up the street, on your right is the former Jesuit College which was turned into a prison in 1803 and later into army barracks. Its immense door (now closed off), dates from the 18th century.

When you arrive at the cathedral, walk around before entering and observe the sculpted heads of fantastic animals as well as masks under the cornices and two large, stone lions. The cathedral of Embrun, dating from the end of the 12th century, reflects the transition between Norman and Gothic styles—huge, somber, yet elegant—with its austere interior accentuating the magnificent stained glass windows. The nave of the cathedral has four vaulted bays on ribbed transept crossings, and the side aisles, with semi-circular vaults, are separated from the nave by pointed archways. Note the high altar in polychrome marble dating from the 18th century, the carved wooden stalls, the great organ, and of course, the majestic rose window. During the summer months the cathedral is also used for classical concerts.

Diagonally across from the cathedral, is the Brown Tower (Tour Brune), dating back to the 13th century. A watch-tower and prison, this was the ancient keep of archbishops. From the back of the cathedral, you can walk up through the park, turning left on any number of streets to reach the main shopping area.

Walk #2: Baratier to Champ de Lare to L'Osselin to Le Poet to Baratier (Excursion to Abbaye de Boscodon)

Walking Easy Time
2½ hours

The Baratier walk is a circular route and brings you from the little village of Baratier at 2874 ft. (876 m.) up to Champ de Lare at 3681 ft. (1122 m.). You will be walking along a country wagon road for an ascent of 328 ft. (100 m.), with views over the lake and the Embrunais. A more challenging uphill climb, on a wide, well-beaten path rising another 492 ft. (150 m.), will bring you to a peaceful country lane past old farms at Champ de Lare and l'Osselin. The walk from Champ de Lare back to Baratier is downhill all the way, through the hamlet of le Poet. The first part of the walk, ascending to Champ de Lare, is more demanding, but the views of the lake and the Embrunais make the climb worth the effort.

With a rest and lunch, plan over four hours for today's outing. There are no facilities or restaurants along the way (except at the beginning and the end of the walk), so put some goodies and water in your backpack along with lunch.

Directions: Take D40 to Baratier and enter off a traffic circle between Embrun and Crots. Make your first right turn and follow signs into Baratier. Parking is usually available in the tiny village center in front of the Post Office.

Start: From the center of the village, across from the little restaurant, walk up the hill on rue de Pouzenc. (If you face the Post Office the street is in back of you.) The path is not marked at this point and is a small, paved country road. Continue walking on this road, bearing to your right, although you might wish to explore the old, narrow streets of the village first. You will begin to see blue-and-yellow blazes on trees, poles or fences as you continue to ascend gently on this road, with views of the lake and the Embrunais below on your right.

Pass barns and homes until you reach a fork in the road with a yellow arrow, confirming your direction straight ahead on Chemin de Verdun. After a short while, a sign directs you more steeply up to your left in the direction of Champ de Lare and l'Osselin. At this point the road also goes to the right past barns and houses, but this is private property, and although your map may show a small walking path through the meadow, do **not** attempt to walk on it. You will be warned off by an irate farmer and his equally irate, barking dogs.

The trail to the left begins to ascend very steeply, but *Easy Walkers* can handle this ascent—do it very slowly, leaning forward into the hill, knowing that the view from the top makes the effort worthwhile.

> ☞ **HINT: Near the top of this climb, use the two little cut-offs on the right to ease your level of ascent.**

When you reach the road at the top, turn right, passing the working farm Champ de Lare and, within a few minutes, l'Osselin with its campground. The barns are ancient, and the green mountains in the background provide a lovely contrast to the sun-drenched fields of grain. Continue around and down on this road, resisting a little signed path to les Vernées. Stay on the quiet, comfortable, country auto road as it zig-zags down the mountain until you reach a blue-and-white sign for les Vernées, off to the left (the second "les Vernées" sign). At this point, follow instead the yellow-blazed arrow onto a descending, rocky, mountain trail. This path brings you down to the road and the little hamlet of le Poet.

Turn right on the road, walking through le Poet, to a four-way intersection signed, "le Poet." One sign directs you to Crots, zig-zagging down a country road to the left. Assuming your car is in Baratier, **walk straight ahead, through the intersection,** past a chalet on your right, le Mélèze. This is a wide, rocky, jeep path, ending at a paved road. Make a left turn on the road, blazed with a yellow arrow, and *voilà*, on the right is the charming sun terrace of the Hotel Peuplies, a pleasant spot to enjoy a cool drink . Continue down the road, making a right turn at the first intersection and walk into the village center of Baratier and your car.

Considering lunch, resting, and scenery-viewing, you should be back in Baratier about four hours after you began today's walk. This might be a good time to visit the Abbaye de Boscodon, completing a gratifying day in the Embrunais. Leave Baratier as you entered this morning, following

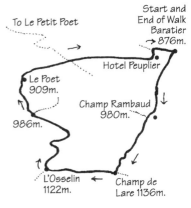

D40 to the main highway and circle, driving three-quarters around the circle towards Crots on N94. Shortly, signs direct you to the left turn to Abbaye de Boscodon. Follow that road directly up to the abbey. This popular attraction is usually crowded and parking can be difficult. There is a second parking area around the circle and to the right.

The abbey was built by the monks 350 years before the discovery of America and is undergoing ongoing restoration, as it did in the 15th, 17th and 18th centuries. Active local and religious groups are in charge of the restoration, while promoting numerous cultural activities at the site. Ninety-minute tours are given in various languages (French, German, Italian and English). Please check with the Tourist Office for the current schedule. The abbey is open to visitors every day from 10:00 am to 7:00 pm.

Walk #3: Excursion to Réallon Chairlift, Walk Réallon to Fortress Ruins to Le Villard to Réallon

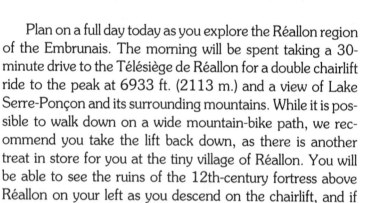

Walking Easy Time
2 hours

Plan on a full day today as you explore the Réallon region of the Embrunais. The morning will be spent taking a 30-minute drive to the Télésiège de Réallon for a double chairlift ride to the peak at 6933 ft. (2113 m.) and a view of Lake Serre-Ponçon and its surrounding mountains. While it is possible to walk down on a wide mountain-bike path, we recommend you take the lift back down, as there is another treat in store for you at the tiny village of Réallon. You will be able to see the ruins of the 12th-century fortress above Réallon on your left as you descend on the chairlift, and if you look closely, you will also see the mountain path you will take later in today's hike.

It will be necessary to drive from Réallon lift station to the village of Réallon to begin today's walk. The first part of the walk to the fortress, an ascent of 656 ft. (200 m.), is a steady climb for about 45 minutes. *Easy Walkers* can handle this ascent provided they take it slowly. The trail down is part of a Grand Randonée route, cutting through grassy, hillside meadows to reach a quiet, country mountain road for the walk back to Réallon. We suggest you take the chairlift portion of today's excursion and walk in the morning, and hike afterwards.

Directions: The drive to Réallon chairlift station is on the far side of the lake and affords new viewing perspectives. Take D94 from Embrun to Savines-le-Lac, crossing the bridge (Pont-de-Savines) and making a right turn in the direction of Réallon. As you climb this narrow, winding, mountain road you will split off to the left in the direction of Réallon Station at the sign. (Later in the day you will drive up the right fork towards Réallon village.) It takes about 30 minutes from Embrun/Crots to the large parking area in front of the lift station. Walk past the hotel to the lift station and purchase a round-trip ticket to the peak.

Take the quiet, 15-minute chairlift ride to the mid-station, with its restaurant, sun terrace and facilities. Walk to the second lift station for another 15-minute ascent to 6933 ft. (2113 m.). The short walk up to the jagged peak affords exciting, close-up views of the "needles" of the Aiguilles de Chabrières.

When you're ready, return to the Réallon base station for

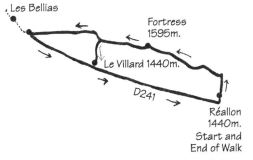

the drive to the village of Réallon. Take the auto road down, just as you came up, making a left turn on the signed fork in the road to Réallon and driving through the picturesque hamlet of les Rousses. The road is a bit narrow and winding, so take it slowly. After entering Réallon, drive through the town until you see a sign on the right reading "Parking" (with an arrow to the right) and "Ruine." Make the sharp right turn up the hill until you reach a parking area at the top of the village. The church steeple will be off to your right.

☞ **HINT: If you are using Embrun Map #3838, note that the village of Réallon is printed on the border of the map above "Station de Réallon." Please note that the walk itself happens to fall on another map, and you should have #3437 "Orcière-Merlette" with you also.**

Start: Walk to the back of the parking area, heading left for a minute, then turning right at the signs directing you to the fort and *ruine*. This rocky, mountain path ascends fairly steeply, and it takes about 45 minutes at a slow pace to reach the ruins—clearly in view in front of you. The climb looks tougher than it is; just lean into the trail, take it very slowly, and you'll reach 5233 ft. (1595 m.) within 45 minutes. A sign indicates that you are at the ruins of a 12th-century fortress—a great place to explore and enjoy a picnic lunch.

When ready, retrace your steps, returning back for a few minutes on the path, blazed white and red, but take the first right turn and walk along the mountainside. The trail narrows as it descends easily along the hillside, with purple flowers in the surrounding meadows, sometimes waist high. The trail is somewhat rocky in spots but easily traversed. The map identifies this trail as GR 50, Tour du Haut Dauphinée. You can see the hamlet of le Villard down on the left. Soon you will come to a descending, rocky stream bed. Turn left and walk down the rocky wagon path taking you to the road at le Villard. Turn left again and walk back on the rarely used road to Réallon and your car.

Walk #4: Les Orres Lift to Top Station, Walk to Petit Vallon and along the Ridge, Return to Les Orres

Walking Easy Time
3 to 5 hours

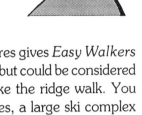

This moderate-level hike at les Orres gives *Easy Walkers* a fresh perspective of the Embrunais, but could be considered more challenging if you go on to take the ridge walk. You will drive to the lift station at les Orres, a large ski complex that services 7000 skiers a day in winter, visited by sports enthusiasts from around France. Now, with the development of Lake Serre-Ponçon, summer visitors are also using the ski facilities, keeping the lifts busy and the trails open.

You will take one of several lifts up to 7874 or 8202 ft. (2400 or 2500 m.), depending on which chairlift is open, and walk up to the peak at 8859 ft. (2700 m.). The paths are wide and easy to find, and a one-hour slow ascent brings you up to the ridge. After exploring the high ridge area between Petit Vallon and Grand Vallon, you can return to les Orres by using one of several options. Allow the better part of the day for this hike and excursion, including travel, lunch, rest and photography. There are facilities at the base and mid-stations of the chairlifts, including restaurants with sun terraces, but a picnic lunch is less expensive and can be just as enjoyable.

Directions: Turn off the main road at the Baratier, les Orres traffic circle, driving in the direction of les Orres Station (not the town of les Orres), on an ascending, winding, mountain road, with lovely views across the valley and back to the lake.

☞ **HINT: Europeans love to take these mountain roads at breakneck speed. If you wish to sightsee, park on one of the wider, inside shoulders, but while driving keep your eyes on the road and your rearview mirror.**

You will soon arrive at les Orres Station, easily recognized by the myriad of high-rise apartments, typical of French ski villages built in the 1950s and '60s. As you enter les Orres Station, take your first available parking spot. Walk through the center of the village, following the signs reading *remontée mécanique*, to the Pré Longis Télésiège, open every day in summer. Buy a ticket to the top station, good for any of the chairlifts in this area. The return is free of charge.

Start: Take the chairlift to the mid-station at 6316 ft. (1925 m.) and exit to one of the two second-station chairlifts that are open that day—either Fontaines or Pousterie. Fontaines will take you to 7819 ft. (2383 m.), while Pousterie rises to 8304 ft. (2531 m.). There are trails to the top ridge visible from both stations. The climb from either lift station takes about one hour to reach le Petit Vallon at 8859 ft. (2700 m.) for a remarkable panorama of Hautes-Alpes peaks. At

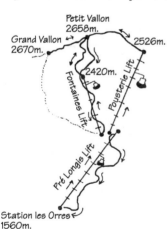

the top, you have the option of walking further towards Grand Vallon at 8760 ft. (2670 m.). The trail is safe, somewhat rocky, with the usual ascents and descents.

Bikers descend from the peak on a variety of trails, and *Easy Walkers* have the following two options: Return by chairlift to the mid-station and take the very visible, wide path down to the base station for an easy descent. Or, follow the biker's path from le Petit Vallon all the way down to the bottom. There is a restaurant with sun terrace and facilities at the mid-station, and as you walk up to the lift station there is also a shaded picnic table under the trees to your left.

Walk #5: Les Pinées to Cascade to Les Pinées

Walking Easy Time
3½ hours

Today *Easy Walkers* have the opportunity to walk mostly in a forest region north of Embrun, close to the village of Châteauroux, and to view a waterfall (la Pisse Cascade). This hike is different than many others in the area because it is on a narrow, sheltered forest trail for most of the way and is generally level. The path is blazed orange, easy to find, and winds under tall pine trees in the cool forest. Your walk will begin at les Pinées after driving from Châteauroux on a narrow, one-lane country road, and it will take about two hours to reach the waterfall, where you will return by the same route. There are no restaurants or facilities along the trail except for the restaurant at the parking area at les Pinées. (Use Orcières-Merlette Map #3437 for this walk.)

Directions: Drive north from Embrun on main road N94 for the short ride into Châteauroux. Make a left turn in the center of the village at a **very hard-to-find sign on the right** for les Pinées. Follow the signs to les Pinées or *refuge* or Auberge les Pinées **(do not follow driving signs to la Cascade)** on a small, winding country road that changes to a bumpy, gravel, one-lane road, ascending to 4265 ft. (1300 m.) at les Pinées. Several side roads take you off to campgrounds and tiny hamlets, but if you stay on the ascending gravel road and follow the above signs, you will reach the parking area next to the inn (*auberge*).

Start: On the side of the inn is an orange-blazed sign directing you to la Cascade. Walk up the wide gravel path for about 984 ft. (300 m.) until you come to a tiny stream. Follow the trail to the right in the direction of la Cascade,

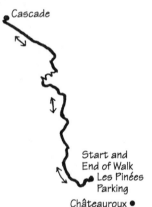

with the canal on your left. This mostly level trail is clearly defined but can be very wet in spots. It soon goes along a small pipeline in the forest that brings water down the mountain and there are occasional leaks. Other signs confirm your direction to la Cascade, and after about 50 minutes, the path descends sharply down to the right, signed again to la Cascade. You will turn left across the stream, taking the path on the right. It is steep for a little bit, but levels out nicely and meets the road to the waterfall. To return, follow the same path back to the parking area at les Pinées.

Walk #6: A Day in the Queyras

Plan a full day for today's walk and excursion

There is a special treat in store for *Easy Walkers* today. Parc Natural Régional du Queyras was first designated in 1977 to preserve the character, rural heritage and natural beauty within 250 square miles of high mountains interspersed with broad, grassy meadows, farms, small villages and hiking trails. But the purpose of our visit today is not only to walk, but also to give *Easy Walkers* the opportunity to experience the simple grandeur that pervades this natural treasure.

You will travel by car from Embrun, through the village of Châteauroux, bypassing Guillestre. The drive is on a narrow, twisting, mountain road through the remarkably beautiful Gorge du Guil. The high, jagged cliffs frame the racing Guil River below, and rafters come from all over the world to ride the Guil rapids. As you enter the heart of the Queyras, the auto road broadens after driving through a few natural mountain tunnels and rises to 4446 ft. (1355 m.) at imposing Château-Queyras—which you will visit on the way back.

Ahead are the villages of Ville-Vieille, Aiguilles, the commercial center of the Queyras, and Abriès. Aiguilles is a small village at 4777 ft. (1456 m.), with a tiny shopping district teeming with French and Italian backpackers (the Italian border is quite close) and an informative Tourist Office. It is a good place to pick up a picnic lunch if you didn't do so earlier. From Aiguilles you will drive on to Abriès, where your walk along the hillside, through the Forêt de Marassan, begins.

You will then return to the village of Ville-Vieille, which you drove through earlier, making a left turn in the direction of Saint-Véran at 6726 ft. (2050 m.), the highest village in Europe. Drive up to the **high** parking area, park, and walk through Saint-Véran, the main tourist attraction of the Queyras. A rare preserved village, the streets of Saint-Véran are bordered by ancient houses, several decorated with sundials painted in the early 19th century. In fact, there are 15 different sundials preserved in Saint-Véran. The architecture in Saint-Véran is distinctive—simple structures of wood and stone, with complimentary roof lines—framed by open meadows and hills.

When ready to leave, return by way of Ville-Vieille back to the 13th-century Château Queyras. Park at the top of the hill, just below the Château. It's fun to wander through the dungeons, along parapets and into army barracks, while crossing drawbridges. Walk through impressively engineered Fort/Château Queyras, but remember, it is easy to get lost in this cavernous building, so it's best to follow the little guide given to you upon entering.

Directions: Today's excursion is split amongst several maps. We recommended that you use the following Michelin driving maps: #245 - Provence, Côte d'Azur; and #244 - Rhône-Alps; and the following hiking map: IGN #3637 - Mont Viso, St-Véran, Aiguilles.

Drive north from Embrun on N94, through Château-roux, turning right on D902 in the direction of Guillestre. Continue on 902 until you branch to the right to Château Queyras, Aiguilles and Abriès on D947. (D902 branches off to the left to Col d'Izoard, climbing on a high serpentine mountain road towards Briançon; this route was made fa-mous by bikers of the Tour de France.) After stopping at Aiguilles, continue on D947 into Abriès. Cross the Torrent de Bouchet (still driving on D947), and as you approach the last group of buildings, make a right turn and park near the Guil River.

Start: Walk across the river and turn right on the path past a shrine. Proceed through the Marassan Forest in the direc-tion of Aiguilles. There is a left turn on a trail that rises up the mountain, but *Easy Walkers* will continue straight ahead along the hillside, walking as far as feels comfortable (remem-bering the forthcoming excursions to St-Véran and Fort

Queyras). The return along the same path provides outstanding views of the high peaks along the Italian border, very close to Abriès. In fact, if you were to walk straight ahead past Ristolas instead of turning left to return to Abriès, you could pick up trail GR58 and cross Col Lacroix into Italy!

Drive back from Abriès as you came, on D947, and at Ville-Vieille turn left on D5 to Saint-Véran. After visiting St-Véran, return to Ville-Vieille on D5, turning left on D947 to Château-Queyras and joining D902 to Guillestre/Mont Dauphin. Return to Embrun on N94.

The following walk was recommended by fellow hikers but not taken by the authors because of time constraints.

Walk #7: The Bouffard Circuit: Saint-André-d'Embrun to Les Chalets de Bouffard to Les Rencuraux to Saint-André-d'Embrun

Walking Easy Time
3½ hours

This walk has an altitude change of 1056 ft. (322 m.) and is blazed in orange. It explores the heights and forests above the tiny hamlet of Saint-André-d'Embrun. It begins on the road going up and out of St-André that receives very little traffic and darts in and out of forests and meadows, through the little village of les Rencuraux to les Esmieux, returning to St-André. If you wish, this walk can be taken in its entirety on the country road.

Directions: Drive through Embrun on N94 (towards Chateauroux), making a right turn at the signs for St-André and Crevoux, continuing down to the river, turning left and then right over the **one-lane** bridge (le Pont Neuf). Turn left and follow the signs into St-André. Park near the church.

Start: Walk past the small town hall and take the path up to the paved road. Cross over the road, walking to the left, until you reach an intersection. Make a right turn here and locate the Saluces forest path. Follow this trail for almost a mile (1½ km). When you arrive at a small pine forest, take the orange-blazed trail to the right and ascend to another forest path. Take this path to the right to les Chalets de Bouffard, and continue on the small road all the way to les Rencuraux. At les Rencuraux take the first road to the right, passing in front of a large farm. Walk past the reservoir to les Esmieux. At a large walnut tree, look to the right and follow the path to a paved road. Bear right and descend into Saint-André-d'Embrun and your car.

PARIS EXPRESS✈ED

"Paris Express✈ed" is written expressly for *Easy Walkers* who wish to spend a few days exploring Paris before or after their alpine walking vacation—using Paris airports for arrival and/or departure. It is **not** intended to be a thorough guide to the City of Light, but rather a "hot list" of important sightseeing attractions.

Most *Walking Easy* readers visit France to walk in the Alps—however, you might wish to add a few extra days to your itinerary for walking in this extraordinarily beautiful and exciting city. If you have only one or two nights to spend in Paris, it might be easier to stay at one of the new, modern (generally less expensive) hotels at the airport, using quick public transportion to and from Paris. Of course, if your itinerary permits more time in Paris, it might be convenient to stay in the city. It is recommended that you purchase one of the many available Paris travel guides to supplement the following information and suggested walking itineraries.

Paris Express✈ed Transportation

By Plane: Roissy/Charles de Gaulle Airport is 15 miles (25 km) northeast of Paris; there are a variety of ways to get to the city from the airport:

> **Roissybus** - Operates every 15 minutes for the 45- to 60-minute ride between the airport and the Opera House on rue Scribe (in central Paris). The bus runs from 6:00 am to 11:00 pm, with stops at Gate 10 in Terminal

2A and Gate 12 in Terminal 2D—these gates servicing Terminals A, B, C and D.

Air France Bus - Departs every 15 to 20 minutes and operates between the airport and Métro stops at Port Maillot and Etoile/Charles de Gaulle (Arc de Triomphe).

Roissyrail - Operates between the airport and central Paris, with important change stops at Gare du Nord and Châtelet-les-Halles (near the Louvre Museum) and Notre-Dame Cathedral.

Orly Airport is 10 miles (16 km) south of Paris. Public transportation from Orly to the city includes:

Orlyval - Take the Orlyval, a frequent (every four to seven minutes) Métro shuttle from Orly Airport, for the quick, synchronized change at Antony to the RER train, Line B, for the 30-minute trip to Châtelet in the center of Paris. At Châtelet there are several options to the Louvre, the Arc de Triomphe and the Champs Elysées.

Air France Bus - With departures every 12 minutes, these buses leave from Orly Airport to les Invalides (Napoléon's Tomb - Hôtel des Invalides) and the Montparnasse train station.

By Métro: The subway trains operate between 5:30 am and 12:30 am and are easy to use and fairly safe (warnings have been issued for pickpockets, however). Each station provides a directional map, and many stations now have "SITU" service, offering a free computer print-out of the best routing and length of the trip.

Within city limits, the same tickets can be used for the métro, RER trains, and buses.

At the station entrance, insert your ticket into the turnstile and walk through. Remember, tickets are sometimes checked at exits and on trains and/or platforms.

In the city one Métro ticket costs 5.50 FF. You also have the option of purchasing the following:

Carnet - 10-ticket packet costs 34.50 FF.

Formule 1 Pass - One day of unlimited travel in zones 1 and 2, cost: 23 FF. The cost is 70 FF for all zones and the two Paris airports. May be used on the Métro, RER trains, buses, SNCF suburban trains and the Montmarte Funicular.

Paris-Visite Pass - This is probably the most economical pass for *Easy Walkers*. It is good for three or five days, can be bought at any Métro ticket counter and allows **unlimited** travel on the Paris métro, bus systems, RER trains and airport connections. These passes are sold at main métro stations and at the Tourist Office on the Champs Elysées. The "Guide Paris Visite" (available in English and French), is an outstanding and informative guidebook, and should accompany the Paris-Visite card.

By Bus: Many first-time visitors to Paris opt to take a get-acquainted bus tour before striking out on their own. Terrific for sightseeing, regular buses run from 6:30 am to about 9:30 pm. You can use your Métro tickets or passes on the bus line, however, buses charge by distance, the Métro does not.

Public Tourist Bus (Balabus/Montmartrobus) - If you are in Paris for the first time on Sunday or a public holiday from noon to 9:00 pm, and want an overview of the city (without commentary), you can take the Balabus and/or the Montmartrobus. The Balabus takes you to the main tourist sites of Paris, with bus stops marked "Balabus Bb." The route from **Place de la Concorde to Gare de Lyon** has stops at Tuileries, Louvre, Palais Royal, Saint Honoré, Pont-Neuf, Notre-Dame, rue du Pont Louis-Philippe, Saint-Paul, place des Vosges and Bastille. The **Gare de Lyon to Place de la Concorde** route stops at Birague, rue Vielle du Temple, Hôtel de Ville, Châtelet, Cité-Palais de Justice, Saint-Michel, Pont-Neuf, Quai de Conti, Pont du Carrousel, Musée d'Orsay and Assemblée Nationale. The Montmartrobus begins at No. 5 on Place Pigalle and runs throughout the Montmarte area, including a stop at Sacré-Coeur.

Cityrama - Double-decker buses leave from 4, place des Pyramides, tel: 42-60-30-14, taking you on a two-hour overview tour of Paris, passing (but not stopping) at the most popular tourist attractions. Earphones in ten languages provide a running commentary, Métro stop: Palais Royal.

Paris Vision - 214, rue de Rivoli, tel: 42-60-31-25, Métro stop: Tuileries; provides bubble-top, double-decker buses with English commentary.

Paris Bus - Leaves from the Eiffel Tower, tel: 42-30-55-50, also provides bubble-top, double-decker buses with English commentary by professional guides.

By Taxi: If the *libre* sign is lit, the cab is available. Do **not** take cabs without meters unless you agree on a fare first. Fares increase at night and weekends, and a 15% tip is customary.

By Boat: The **Batobus** operates on the Seine River from April to September, stopping at locations near the Eiffel Tower, the Louvre, Notre-Dame, etc. Look for signs on the quays. You can enjoy many of the best views of Notre-Dame and the bridges and riverside areas on a **Bateaux Mouches** cruise on the Seine. The boats leave from the right bank of the Seine next to Pont de l'Alma, tel: 42-25-96-10, Métro stop:Alma-Marceau. **Les Bateaux Parisiens**, Pont d'Iéna, tel: 47-05-50-00; and **Vedettes Pont-Neuf**, place Vert-Galant, tel: 46-33-93-38, also provide glass-enclosed boats to navigate the Seine River, presenting an ever-changing picture of the city.

Paris Express→ed Activities and Attractions

The main Paris Tourist Information Office (Office du Tourisme) is located at 127 Champs Elysées and is open daily from 9:00 am to 8:00 pm. *Easy Walkers* should pick up a city map, a public transportation map, brochures with current museum hours and costs, "Paris Information" (a tourist magazine written in English), and discount museum passes and transportation cards. Allo Bonjour is a service provided by the French Tourism Ministry and the Paris Convention Visitors Bureau. If you dial 49-52-53-54 between 9:00 am and 8:00 pm you can access a multilingual information line.

1. Centre National d'Art et de Culture Georges Pompidou - place Georges-Pompidou - Named for the French president who decided to create this cultural center, the innovative skeletal outer structure sits in the middle of a large, pedestrians-only area and now draws more visitors than the Eiffel Tower! The Center is made up of the **Musée d'Art Moderne (National Museum of Modern Art)** and its collection of 20th-century modern art masterpieces; the **Public Information Library** with free access to over one million books, periodicals, etc.; the **Institute for Research and Coordination of Acoustics/Music**, primarily for musicians and composers; and the **Center for Industrial Design**. The center is open Monday and Wednesday to Friday from noon to 10:00 pm, Saturday and Sunday from 10:00 am to 10:00 pm, and admission is charged.

Métro stop: Rambuteau, Hôtel-de-Ville

2. Musée d'Orsay - 1, rue de Bellechasse - A former train station has been transformed into a great museum of 19th-century art, and its impressionist section continues to draw large crowds. Don't miss the incredible van Gogh paintings displayed on the top floor—just one section of its 80 different galleries with furniture, photography, objets d'art, and of course, its celebrated paintings. The museum is closed Mondays, but is open Tuesday, Wednesday and Friday to Sunday from 10:00 am to 6:00 pm, Thursday from 10:00 am to 9:15 pm. Admission is charged.

Métro stop: Solférino

3. Basilica of Sacré-Coeur - place St-Pierre - The Montmarte section of Paris, location of Sacré-Coeur, was the artists' area of Paris in the late 19th and early 20th centuries, its night scenes immortalized in the paintings of Toulouse-Lautrec. The shining white-domed church, located on the highest of the seven hills of Paris, was built in the late 1800s. Its interior in rich Byzantine style, the view from its dome extends almost 35 miles in every direction. The basilica is open daily from 7:00 am to 11:00 pm, the dome and crypt daily from 9:00 am to 7:00 pm. Admission is charged to the dome and crypt; the basilica is free.

Métro stop: Abbesses or Anvers

4. Le Forum des Halles - The central market of Paris was razed in 1969, and 80 acres of trendy shops, theaters, galleries and restaurants, mostly underground, have been built in a contemporary steel and glass structure. For many people, a bowl of traditional French onion soup at a les Halles restaurant is the only way to end a night on the town. **Métro stop: Les Halles**

5. Musée Picasso - Hôtel Salé 5, rue de Thorigny - The Hôtel Salé is a 17th-century mansion located in the oldest area of Paris, and it houses the greatest Picasso collection in the world as well as Picasso's own collection of works by other famous artists. The museum is open daily except Tuesday from 9:15 am to 5:15 pm, Wednesday evenings until 10:00 pm, with admission charge. **Métro stop: St-Paul or Chemin-Vert**

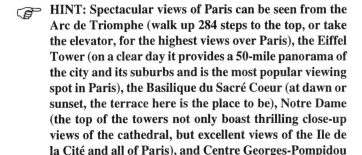

☞ **HINT: Spectacular views of Paris can be seen from the Arc de Triomphe (walk up 284 steps to the top, or take the elevator, for the highest views over Paris), the Eiffel Tower (on a clear day it provides a 50-mile panorama of the city and its suburbs and is the most popular viewing spot in Paris), the Basilique du Sacré Coeur (at dawn or sunset, the terrace here is the place to be), Notre Dame (the top of the towers not only boast thrilling close-up views of the cathedral, but excellent views of the Ile de la Cité and all of Paris), and Centre Georges-Pompidou (note the fabulous panorama from the landing at the top of the escalator).**

Paris Express→ed Excursions

Most sightseeing areas around Paris can be reached by train, but because of time constraints, a car is a more viable travel option, enabling *Easy Walkers* to visit more areas in a shorter period of time.

1. Versailles - The opulent palace of Versailles, one of the greatest monuments to lavish living (its cost nearly bank-rupted France!), is 13 miles southwest of Paris. Building was started in 1661 and progressed over 50 years. In the mid-19th century, after Napoleon's victories, Versailles was converted to a museum "dedicated to the glory of France."

Versailles is composed of three main areas: the **palace** with its six magnificent **Grands Appartements**, the **gardens**, and the **Trianons**. The most famous room in the palace is probably the **Hall of Mirrors**, 236 feet long with 17 large windows and reflecting mirrors. The **gardens** of Versailles cover 250 acres, originally with 1400 fountains. A walk across the gardens brings you to the palaces of the **Grand Trianon** and **Petit Trianon**. Between the Trianon palaces is a **carriage museum** with coaches from the 18th and 19th centuries.

The apartments, chapel, and Hall of Mirrors can be visited without a guide Tuesday to Sunday from 9:45 am to 5:00 pm, with admission charge. Other areas can be seen with a guide on specific days. The palace is closed Monday and holidays. The Trianons are open Tuesday to Sunday from 9:45 am to noon and 2:00 to 5:00 pm, and admission is charged.

Fireworks and illuminated fountains can be seen on many summer evenings. Check with the Tourist Office for current information, dates and seat prices.

Directions: By car - Take route N10 to Versailles and park in front of the palace. By Métro - Exit at Pont de Sèvres station and transfer to bus #171, stopping near the palace gates. The trip takes about 15 minutes. By train - Take RER line C5, leaving every 15 minutes from Paris to Versailles-Rive Gauche. Turn right when you exit the station.

2. Fountainebleau - The Palace of Fountainebleau, called by Napoleon the "house of the centuries," lies 37 miles south of Paris. It was originally used as a hunting resort in the wooded forest and under François I grew into a royal palace. Some of the more outstanding rooms in the palace are the

Gallery of François I, the **ballroom** and the **Napoleonic rooms**, along with the **Louis XV staircase**.

You can enjoy most of the palace on your own, but the Napoleonic rooms are open by guided tour only. The apartments are open Wednesday through Monday from 9:30 am to 12:30 pm and 2:00 pm to 5:00 pm, with admission charge. Outside the palace, walk through the **gardens** and around the carp pond.

Directions: By car - Follow A6 out of Paris towards Lyon, exiting at Fountainebleau. By train and bus - Trains leave from Gare de Lyon in Paris and take 35 minutes to one hour. The station is outside of town in Avon—a local bus makes the two-mile drive to the château every 15 minutes Monday to Saturday and every 30 minutes on Sunday.

3. Chartres - Sixty miles southwest of Paris, the medieval **Cathédrale de Notre-Dame de Chartres**, third-largest in the world, has become known as the "stone testament of the middle ages." Its architecture, sculpture and, most of all, its stained glass, give new meaning to these art forms of so long ago. Even before entering the cathedral, the Romanesque sculptures of the **royal portal** reportedly mesmerized Rodin for hours. The **nave** is broader than any in France, its ogival arches rising to 122 feet. The **Clocher Vieux (Old Tower) steeple** dates back to the 12th century, and the **Clocher Neuf (New Tower)** is from 1134.

The royal portal was added in the 12th century, and inside the church is a famous **choir screen**, created between the 16th and 18th centuries. However, it is the extraordinary **stained glass windows** that seem to transfix most visitors, like a kaleidoscope, they never look the same as the sun moves across the sky. The **crypt**, third-largest in the world and the oldest part of the cathedral, was built from the 9th to the 11th centuries. A walk through the **Episcopal gardens** will give you yet another perspective on this remarkable sight.

You can visit daily at 11:00 am, 2:00, 3:15 and 4:30 pm; admission is charged. Make a reservation at the south portal at la Crypt. The cathedral itself is open daily from 7:00 am to 7:00 pm.

Directions: By car - Drive to Chartres, 60 miles southwest of Paris. By train - Trains run to Chartres from the Gare Montparnasse and take less than an hour.

Paris Express→ed Walks

Walk #1: Place de l'Opera to Rue de la Paix to Place Vendôme to Place de la Concorde to Musée de l'Orangerie to Tuileries Gardens to Louvre Museum to Notre-Dame Cathedral

Walk or take the Métro (Opéra stop) to **place de l'Opéra**. Walk away from the world's largest opera house and turn right on the fashionable shopping street, rue de la Paix, to **place Vendôme**, one of the loveliest squares in Paris. Designed in the 17th century, it is now a walking-only area, its arcaded shops containing jewelers, perfumers, banks, the Ministry of Justice, and the Ritz Hotel.

Walk through Vendôme and pick up rue Castiglione to rue Rivoli. Cross over Rivoli straight ahead to enter the **Tuileries Gardens**—one of the finest examples of French formal gardens, designed by the man who planned the gardens at Versailles—laid out in geometric shapes with shrubbery, formal flower beds, statues and fountains.

A right turn brings you to **Jeu de Paume**, a gallery of contemporary art facing place de la Concorde. It is closed on Monday and open irregular hours the rest of the week, with an admission charge; call 47-03-12-50 for information. Across the gardens from the Jeau de Paume is **Musée de l'Orangerie**, with magnificent paintings by Cézanne,

Renoir, Utrillo, Rousseau, Picasso and others. The museum is open Wednesday to Monday from 9:45 am to 5:15 pm, with admission charge.

Turn right on the main walking path in the gardens (between the Jeau de Paume and the Orangerie Museum) to the **Louvre Museum** entrance, **la Pyramide**, designed by I.M. Pei. The entrance to the Louvre is through this controversial 71-foot-high glass pyramid, housing a collection of shops and restaurants and automatic ticket machines.

The two most famous ladies of the Louvre Museum, the Venus de Milo sculpture and Leonardo da Vinci's Mona Lisa, draw the crowds, but familiar masterpieces are commonplace in this treasure trove. The museum is divided into six departments: Egyptian, Oriental, Greek and Roman antiquities, sculpture, painting, and furniture and art objects. With 200 galleries covering 40 acres and almost 300,000 items in its collections, many days are needed to fully appreciate the world's largest museum!

Guided tours in English, covering the highlights of the Louvre, are available. Check for information and purchase tickets at the window marked "Acceuil des Groupes," located inside the Pyramid. The museum is open Thursday to Sunday from 9:00 am to 6:00 pm, Monday and Wednesday from 9:00 am to 9:45 pm, and admission is charged.

Exit the Louvre onto the banks of the Seine and walk along the river, crossing at its oldest bridge, **Pont Neuf**. The Seine forks here to form **Ile de la Cité**, actually the birthplace of Paris about 250 B.C. Turn left as soon as you cross the first fork of the river and walk straight ahead to the Conciergerie, the remains of the former royal palace, used as a prison during the French Revolution. It is open daily from 10:00 am to 6:30 pm, with admission charge.

In back of the **Conciergerie** is la Sainte-Chapelle and the **Palais de Justice**. The Gothic architecture of **Sainte Chapelle** was originally conceived to house the Sacred

Crown of Thorns and other holy relics sent from Constantinople in the 13th century. Note the brilliant stained-glass windows, with more than a thousand miniature scenes of biblical life, and the graceful 247-foot church spire. Sainte-Chapelle is open daily from 9:30 am to 6:00 pm, admission charge.

Exiting the church, walk straight ahead into Place du Parvis de Notre Dame. Distances from Paris to all parts of France are measured from a plaque in the center of this square. **Cathédrale Notre-Dame de Paris** is located on the front of the square on this island in the Seine, rich in history and historical monuments. To better appreciate one of the world's finest examples of Gothic architecture, first walk around the entire building. The foundations for the cathedral were laid in 1163, and it took more than 200 years to build, with sculptured portals, graceful columns, splendid stained-glass windows (best viewed at sunset), choir screens, altars, paintings and sculptures.

Victor Hugo immortalized the cathedral in "The Hunchback of Notre Dame," and to visit the famous gargoyles you can walk up the steps leading to 225-foot-high, twin, square towers—flat on top. Perhaps you can visualize Quasimodo peering from behind one of those grimy, grotesque stone sculptures! The cathedral is open daily from 8:00 am to 7:00 pm, except during Sunday mass; its treasury is open Monday to Saturday from 10:00 am to 6:00 pm, Sunday 2:00 pm to 6:00 pm; the gargoyles can be seen daily from 10:00 am to 4:30 pm. Admission to the cathedral is free, but there is a charge to see the treasury and the gargoyles.

Walk through the garden in back of the cathedral to the end of Île de la Cité for a view of the **Memorial to the Deportation**, in memory of French martyrs of the underground resistance of World War II who were deported to concentration camps. It is open from 10:00 am to noon and 2:00 pm to 7:00 pm, and admission is free.

Between Notre-Dame and the Church of Sainte-Chapelle is the Cité Métro stop with its art deco entrance.

Walk #2: Eiffel Tower to École Militaire to Les Invalides (Napoléon's Tomb) to Rodin Museum to Petit Palais (Museum of Fine Arts of Paris) to Grand Palais to Champs Elysées

Walk or take the Métro (Bir-Hakeim or Trocadéro stop) to **le Tour Eiffel**. This symbol of the Paris skyline, built in 1889, is one of the most recognizable structures in the world. The tower is 1056 feet high and on a clear day the incredible views from the top span a radius of over 40 miles. The elevator to the first landing provides views of the rooftops of Paris, and here you will find a movie, museum, restaurants and bar; the second landing gives you a view of the city; the third stage boasts an incredible panorama of Paris with its monuments and the surrounding countryside. The Tower is open daily from 9:30 am to 11:00 pm, admission is charged according to floor.

After leaving the Eiffel Tower, walk through **Champ de Mars** park with trees, gardens, reflecting pool, and fountains, to **École Militaire**, established in 1751 by King Louis XV for needy officers-in-training—now a defense study center. Facing the school and just beyond it is the main **UNESCO** building, erected in 1958 and decorated with frescoes by Picasso, mobiles by Calder, murals by Miró, Japanese gardens by Noguchi and sculpture by Henry Moore.

Turn left past UNESCO on ave. de Ségur and walk ahead to place Vauban and straight ahead to **les Invalides** and **Napoléon's Tomb**. This vast building was built by Louis XIV as a refuge for disabled soldiers and contains ten miles of corridors under its golden dome. The royal Church of the

Dôme, part of the complex, houses the Tomb of Napoleon. Also part of les Invalides is an Army Museum containing weapons, uniforms and equipment. The complex is open daily from 10:00 am to 6:00 pm.

Passing Eglise du Dôme and the Court of Honor, you can detour to the **Musée Rodin**, located in an 18th-century Paris home. Many of Rodin's sculptures are placed throughout the elegant gardens. It is open daily except Monday from 10:00 am to 5:45 pm, with admission charge. To reach the Rodin Museum, turn right on place des Invalides, right on boulevard des Invalides and left on rue de Varennes. The museum is on the right.

Walk back and cross place des Invalides, now walking on ave. W. Churchill, crossing the Seine on Pont Alexandre III. On the right is the **Petit Palais - Museum of Fine Arts of Paris**, containing exhibits of Paris history along with early painting and sculpture. The museum is open daily except Monday from 10:00 am to 5:45 pm; admission is charged.

Across from the Petit Palais is the **Grand Palais**, built for the 1900 World Exposition. It is now the home of the Paris Science Museum and Planetarium and is open from 10:00 am to 8:00 pm daily except Tuesday, with admission charge.

There is a Métro stop (Pl. Clemenceau) where ave. W. Churchill meets the Champs Elysées.

Walk #3: Arc de Triomphe to the Champs Elysées to Place de la Concorde to Madeleine Church to Place de l'Opera

Walk or take the Métro (Charles-de-Gaulle/Etoile stop) to the **Arc de Triomphe**, the largest and probably most famous triumphal arch in the world—163 feet high and 147 feet wide—located at the western end of the Champs Elysées. It was commissioned by Napoléon to commemorate his victories, and beneath the Arc is the Tomb of the Unknown Soldier and the Eternal Flame. The view of Paris from the top is extraordinary, and you can take the elevator or climb the stairs. The Arc de Triomphe is open daily from 10:00 am to 6:00 pm.

Twelve broad avenues, including the Champs-Elysées, radiate from the Arc like spokes on a wheel. To reach the Arc and/or the Champs Elysées, use the underground passage—do not attempt to cross the busy square on city streets!

Walk on the **Champs Elysées** from the Arc de Triomphe and place de l'Étoile, past Rond-Point. Mark Twain wrote that the Champs-Elysées was the liveliest street in the world. Today you will find high-priced sidewalk cafés, tourist stores and even fast-food hamburger places. However, the broad, tree-lined boulevard stretches for two miles and is still a great place for window shopping or people-watching.

Turn left on ave. de Marigny and right on rue du Faubourg St. Honoré, passing the **Elysée Palace**, residence of the President of France. This street is noted for the chic boutiques of high fashion designers.

Turn left on rue Royale and walk to place de la Madeleine and **Church of the Madeleine**, built in 1806 by Napoléon to honor his fighting men. Note the 34-foot-high bronze doors depicting the Ten Commandments.

At the front of place de la Madeleine, turn diagonally right and enter blvd. de la Madeleine, strolling onto one of the grand boulevards of Paris, and then entering place de l'Opera. If you turn right on to rue de la Paix you can enjoy some expensive Paris shopping, but if you turn left and walk two blocks, you will find the department stores Galeries Lafayette and Printemps. The imposing Rococo Paris **Opera House** is located to the left on the square. Its ornate interior, including a famous Chagall dome, is open daily from 11:00 am to 4:30 pm, admission charge.

The nearest Métro stops to the Opera House are: Opera (in the square) or R.E.R. Auber (on rue Auber, past the American Express office).

ACCOMMODATIONS

The following reasonably priced hotels are used by the authors on their walking trips. All rooms have private facilities, include continental breakfast (unless otherwise indicated), and are comfortable, scrupulously clean, and well-located. Most hotels are family-owned and justifiably proud of their kitchens. For an expanded list of hotels, contact the individual Tourist Office of each village you plan to visit.

Remember, when calling or faxing France, the international access number from the United States is always **011 33**, followed by the listed telephone or fax number.

☞ **HINT: The recommended accommodations ALL accept credit cards.**

AVALLON

Le Relais Fleuri
Three-star; Owner Familie Schiever
89200 Yonne (Avallon)
Tel: 86-34-02-85, Fax: 86-34-09-98

Le Relais Fleuri is a member of the Logis de France group of hotels and is located off the main A6 route between Paris and Lyon, in a park-like setting near the historic town of Avallon. Its swimming pool and pleasant gardens can offer a welcome respite after a trans-Atlantic flight; the hotel is only two to three hours driving time from Paris. Traditional French Burgundy cuisine is served in the hotel's restaurant.

BOURG-SAINT-MAURICE/LES ARCS

L'Autantic Hotel
Three-star; Owner Angele Bourgeois
Route d'Hauteville, 73700 Bourg-Saint-Maurice
Tel: 79-07-01-70, Fax: 79-07-51-55

L'Autantic Hotel is a new, pine and fieldstone chalet, sitting in a large, grassy meadow away from the traffic of Bourg-Saint-Maurice, yet only a few minutes' drive to the center of the village. The amenities are very comfortable and modern, all 23 bedrooms with private facilities. This is a bed and breakfast, giving *Easy Walkers* the opportunity to sample the local cuisine at some of the village restaurants. As of this writing, l'Autantic is the only three-star hotel in Bourg-Saint-Maurice.

Gran Paradiso Hotel Mercure
Three-star; part of the Mercure hotel chain
Arc 1800, Charmettoger, 73700 Les Arcs
Tel: 79-07-65-00, Fax: 79-07-64-08

This modern hotel, located on the mountain at Arc 1800, is the newest hotel in les Arcs. A large hotel with 81 rooms, all equipped with ultra-modern private facilities, balconies and mini-bars, it offers superb views of the surrounding mountains. This is a top-notch, full-service, quality hotel with evening entertainment, bar, reception rooms, and full restaurant with terrace—and all the know-how of the Mercure chain. Their demi-pension summer prices are very attractive, and since most of the walking is on the mountain in the les Arcs area, this hotel offers *Easy Walkers* a viable alternative to staying down in Bourg-Saint-Maurice. Evenings are sure to be cooler at les Arcs since it is 3300 ft. (1000 m.) higher than Bourg-Saint-Maurice in the valley.

CHAMONIX

Hotel La Sapinière
Three-star; Owner Familie Cachat
102, rue Mummery, B.P. 85, 74402 Chamonix-Mont Blanc
Tel: 50-53-07-63, Fax: 50-53-10-14

This superbly run hotel is in a quiet location, a five-minute walk from the center of Chamonix. An inviting terrace and shaded gardens surround the hotel; inside is a bar and lounge for after-dinner drinks and conversation. The 30 hotel rooms all face south for views of the glacier, and the Cachat family had the foresight to donate the meadow in front of the hotel to the town as a green belt, thus ensuring that nothing can be built to destroy the view!

Jeanne and Alain Cachat take great pride in their establishment, originally built in the 1920s and renovated in 1962 and 1968. The Cachats were one of Chamonix's founding families, arriving as farmers in 1650, with Alain Cachat a third-generation hotelier.

The kitchen is excellent and a full buffet breakfast is served, including orange juice, corn flakes, soft-boiled eggs (on request), yoghurt, cheeses, cold meats, bread and rolls, and hot beverages. Excellent dinners includes soup, choice of appetizer, main course, and an array of delectable desserts with fresh fruit always available. The chef has been in charge of the kitchen at La Sapinière for 25 years and is a master of French cuisine, however the accommodating staff will always cater to special needs if notified in advance.

La Sapinière is a favorite hotel because of the quality of the food and service, the location, the view, and the friendly and helpful atmosphere created by American-born Jeanne and Chamonix-born Alain Cachat.

EMBRUN

Hotel Les Bartavelles
Three-star; Owner Familie Jaume
05200 Crots
Tel: 92-43-20-69, Fax: 92-43-11-92

Les Bartavelles is a few kilometres from Embrun and sits on a grassy meadow near the village of Crots. There are well-maintained tennis courts and an outdoor swimming pool, making this hotel a comfortable family resort on several acres, in a park-like setting. Rooms are available with or without balconies in the main building, while other rooms are available in satellite buildings on the grounds.

Unlike the high, northern Alps of France, the Embrun area is in high season in summer due to the attractions of Lake Serre-Ponçon, and reservations may be more difficult to obtain. The owners make every effort to provide activities for their guests, however the kitchen (in the summer of '94) is just average. The hotel is 30 years old, and room furnishings, while spotlessly clean, could use an updating.

La Grande Ferme
Gites de France; Owners Familie Vergnolle
les Rauffes, 05200 Saint André d'Embrun
Tel: 92-43-09-99

The authors fell in love with this grand old barn that has been remodeled into a small, charming mountainside hotel. Each of the rooms, some with spacious apartments with kitchens, include modern, private facilities and have a typical chalet feeling with exposed beams and pine panelling. The restaurant, originally home to the farm animals, has a reputation for typical French country cooking, and its romantic atmosphere is enhanced by its cave-like setting with low, vaulted stone ceilings. This hotel sits on a hillside less than four miles (6 km) from Embrun, overlooking the countryside, the mountains and the "rock of Embrun." If reservations are available, and if you don't mind those extra few minutes driving into town, this is a great choice for *Easy Walkers*. The young owners speak English, and you'd better reserve early.

Le Réal
Owners Iain and Sue Davidson
Quartier de Pont Frache, 05200 Embrun
Tel: 92-43-46-94, Fax: 92-43-54-47

Iain and Sue Davidson, originally from the British Isles, have recently become part of Embrun. They offer a very comfortable, traditional alpine home, with spectacular mountain views, that has recently been converted into self-catering apartments. Each apartment has a living area, a dining area, and fully equipped kitchen, as well as private facilities. This small chalet is set in a garden with ample car parking, just a few minutes from Embrun center. *Easy Walkers* might enjoy these surroundings, supervised by the Davidsons who are avid walkers and who can be helpful with all facets of an Embrun walking vacation. Early reservations are a necessity—we think you will enjoy these intimate surroundings.

MEGÈVE

Hotel La Grange d'Arly
Three-star; Owner Familie Allard
B.P. 68, rue des Allobroges, 74120 Megève
Tel: 50-58-77-88, Fax: 50-93-07-13

Recently built in 1990, this chalet-style hotel is attractively decorated in "country French," using much wood, colorful print fabrics and traditional Savoyarde furniture—both in its downstairs public rooms and its large, comfortable bedrooms, with modern bathrooms and outside balconies. La Grange d'Arly is located away from the village center, near the bus terminal and Sports Center, yet only a quick, five-minute walk into town.

The young owners, Christine and Jean-Marie Allard, take pains to make you feel very much at home, as though you were visiting in their home instead of a full-service, 24-room hotel. They speak English and can help you find everything and anything you may need on your visit to Megève.

Continental breakfast, with complimentary newspaper, can be taken in your room or downstairs in the sunny, attractive dining room. It consists of orange juice, butter and jam, coffee or tea, and a sumptuous basket of French bread, croissants and pastry. Soft-boiled eggs are available on request. Since the summer of '94, dinner is also available to guests at a demi-pension rate, if desired. Prepared by Mme. Allard, it is French home cooking at its best—an appetizer, main course (such as *coq au vin*), cheese course, and dessert and/or fresh fruit—a simple yet delicious ending to a day of walking or sightseeing.

MERIBEL

Hotel Allodis
Three-star; Owner Familie Front
Le Belvédère, B.P. 43 F, 73550 Méribel
Tel: 79-00-56-00, Fax: 79-00-59-28

The Hotel Allodis is a truly exceptional three-star hotel with a five-star kitchen and amenities, a caring staff, and owners who will help make your *Walking Easy* vacation in Méribel a *belle* experience. The chalet-hotel, designed and built in 1988 by a well-known local architect, is in le Belvédère, the newest and highest area in Méribel—situated against the ski runs and overlooking a marvelous panorama of mountains and forests. Although the road ends at the Hotel Allodis, a convenient Méribus stop is outside the front door, taking summer walkers to every section of Méribel, from the Altiport to Méribel Centre to the lifts on the hillside in Méribel-Mottaret.

Boasting modern amenities—indoor swimming pool, half-court tennis, sauna, fitness room, game room and lovely gardens and sun terrace—the Hotel Allodis was headquarters for CBS during the Albertville Winter Olympics. Its 43 bedrooms and the public rooms are decorated in Savoie-contemporary style, making extensive use of traditional pine furniture and moldings, blending with contemporary fabrics and fixtures. In addition to the spacious bedrooms, all with balcony and view of the mountains, the hotel includes one large apartment and 22 mixed suites, some with lofts, fireplaces and sitting rooms.

A typical French continental breakfast is served in the cheerful breakfast room, or if you prefer, in your room. Dinner is no less than a gastronomic experience, beginning with crisp Porthault linens, flowered Limoges/Porthault porcelain and lovely floral arrangements. The demi-pension menu is composed of an appetizer, main course, assortment of cheeses and dessert, accompanied by freshly baked rolls—every dish artfully composed to increase the sensory experience.

A typical dinner might begin with a mixed green salad topped with freshly caught fish from Lake Geneva, then grilled duck breast served on a bed of homemade noodles with a garnish of baby carrots and miniature zucchini, a selection of local cheeses is next, and to top it off, perhaps an artfully arranged, edible cookie basket filled with intensely flavored sorbet and a mixture of fresh fruit, all surrounded by the essence of pureed berries! The description does not do justice to the taste and visual appeal of this chef's creations.

INDEX TO WALKS

INDEX

Our books are available in many bookstores. If you have difficulty finding them, you can order directly from Gateway Books by sending check or money order to:

Gateway Books, 2023 Clemens Road, Oakland CA 94602

Walking Easy in the Austrian Alps $10.95......................... _____

Walking Easy in the French Alps $11.95...........................,_____

Walking Easy in the Italian Alps $11.95...........................,_____

Walking Easy in the San Francisco Bay Area $11.95....... _____

Walking Easy in the Swiss Alps $10.95...............................,_____

> Postage & Handling
> First book............................$1.90
> Each additional book..........1.00
> **California residents add 8% sales tax**

Total $ _____

( ) I enclose my check or money order
( ) Please charge my credit card

Visa   Master Card   American Express

#_____Exp. Date _____

Name on Card _____

Telephone   (   )_____

Please ship to:

Name_____

Address _____

City/State/Zip_____

Our books are shipped bookrate. Please allow 2 - 3 weeks for delivery. If you are not satisfied, the price of the book(s) will be refunded in full. (U. S. funds for all orders, please.)

We want your comments, your criticisms and your suggestions of additional walks, excursions and accommodations to include in future editions. Please mail them to us at 2023 Clemens Road, Oakland, CA 94602, fax them to (510) 530-0497 or e-mail them to donmerwin@aol.com

Notes